Pedagogy of Science
at Secondary Level

Pedagogy of Science
at Secondary Level

Baiju K Nath

SHIPRA

₹ 850; US$ 42.50
ISBN: 978-93-86262-81-3

First Published in India in 2018

Pedagogy of Science
at Secondary Level

Published by:
SHIPRA PUBLICATIONS
LG 18-19, Pankaj Central Market
I.P. Ext., Patparganj, Delhi 110092, India
Tel.: +91 11 2223 5152/6152
E-mail: info@shiprapublication.com
www.shiprapublication.com

Contents

UNIT 1

Learner at Secondary Level

Psychological Considerations

CHAPTER 1
Stages of Cognitive Development

Jean Piaget, a Swiss psychologist conducted many experiments in the area of cognitive development and formulated the basic concepts and four stages of cognitive development.

According to him, cognitive ability of a child directly depends on the cognitive developmental stage of a child. So, as teachers we should understand the basic concepts of cognitive development and its implications to class room learning. It is also necessary to understand the stage of cognitive development of secondary level pupils.

Cognitive Development — Important Considerations by Piaget

There are various processes behind the act of knowing. But, one task of psychology is to describe the cognitive processes behind knowing. These cognitive processes are changing progressively with the childhood age to adult stage.

According to Piaget, adult intelligence derives from the sensori motor coordination in infants, through a series of stages that are related to age. The basic concepts of Piagetian theory of cognitive development are given below.

Adaptation

The living things develop adaptation, which derives in accordance with the environment. This acquisition must be necessary to lead a successful life in their environment. We know that the acquisition of desirable characteristics are otherwise known as adaptation. Each child exhibits a variety of adaptive behaviour similar to that of animals, during the course of its growth and development to an adult stage. According to Piaget, the adaptation process includes two specific processes namely, assimilation and accommodation.

Assimilation: It is interesting to watch small babies. Their only means of communication is crying during the initial months. This helpless condition is gradually transforms as the child grows and develops to laugh, speak, hold objects, sit and walk. These different activities help the child to receive different forms of sensations from all types of external concrete environment. These sensations lead to gradual mental development of the child in due course.

This development takes place by understanding and internalising the various objects in the surrounding. It is a process of familiarisation.

Say for example, you might, have seen that small babies take any object and put it into their mouth, in order to familiarize it, and also to learn or familiarise with the process of eating. Here the process of eating develops as a new behaviour to the existing reflex action, such as sucking. But, the child does not know which all objects are eatable. While s/he is putting every object into mouth, the child understands which all are eatable. And also s/he can gradually recognise the specific taste of different materials.

It is the same process, which happens in writing also. While the child plays with different objects, s/he learns to hold things correctly. This ability helps the child to hold pencils or pens in future. Thus, playing with objects helps the children to familiarise with holding pencils or pens for writing.We teach children to draw lines and dots in zig-zag manner before introducing the letters. Then we may give letters and pictures to children in dotted form and ask them to draw between the dots to get a complete letter or a picture. Why do we do this? Is there any difference in teaching letters directly or in the way we have seen above?

Accommodation: We have already seen how children understand various processes in life. When the child realises that all objects are not eatable, s/he manages to play with the objects which are not edible. Many similar processes are found in our daily life.

We have also seen how children learn to write letters. A child at this stage may be in confusion at first, if s/he is asked to write a word from the known letters. We can see that, by encouragement, a child finally succeeds in writing a word. Here the child adjusts with the new situation.Children at the beginning stage of speaking would have a habit of repeating whatever the family members speak. Through this repetition process, the child understands how to speak. A child at this stage would come across many puzzling situations. For instance, if we asked her/him to tell father's name, s/he may get puzzled and would say that "my father's name is father". Actually the child does not know the name, but in order to meet with the reality s/he makes an adjustment. This process of changing the existing category of knowledge to adjust with reality is referred to as 'accommodation' by Piaget. Accommodation in children would be having very strong influence in their thinking process.

So, adaptation with the environment is an integration of assimilation and accommodation.

Equilibration

The interaction between assimilation and accommodation helps for adjustments with the environment. Along with the interaction, a balance between these two processes is necessary. Let us see how this balance is established. Say for example, crow may be the first bird familiar to young children. Any bird, which could fly is a crow to the children at this stage. This is a wrong assimilation. But s/he might have also assimilated the 'Cro.. Cro' sound of the crow. When s/he sees a hen which does not make 'Cro.. Cro' sound s/he is puzzled. And therefore, s/he is ready to accommodate by receiving new knowledge about the new bird (here hen).

As the child grows and develops, s/he will face situations in which existing knowledge is insufficient for the adjustment. Thus, a state of confusion namely disequilibrium is created. This disequilibrium in turn triggers a process of self regulation namely, equilibration. We have seen that adaptation takes place through assimilation and accommodation. One could adapt with the new situation only if s/he is ready to assimilate and accommodate the new knowledge. Here, equilibration acts as the self regulatory process by helping each one to adjust with the new situation that is to get relieved from disequilibrium. The equilibration stage is not a static stage. It changes to a state of disequilibrium when the child meets with a new puzzling situation. This disequilibrium motivates the child to assimilate and accommodate which leads to the progressive development of the child.

Raju is three years old, who sees an elephant for the first time. Suddenly a disequilibrium develops and tempts him to ask, "What is it?" His father may say, 'Elephant.' After a moment of equilibration disequilibrium occurs, when he looks at the elephant part by part. And at last he gets the full concept of elephant through repeated equilibration, while getting satisfactory answers for his questions.

Conservation

We are living in a world where all sorts of comparison can happen. We can compare objects on the basis of their size, arrange them in order and also able to count numbers. These abilities gradually develop while children are growing. These developments are based on another cognitive process namely conservation. Let us examine some examples.

Example 1: Usually children at the kindergarten stage cry for big pencils. This is the indication that they have conservation of size. If you give them a full sized pencil, they will stop crying. Otherwise they may cry till their aim is attained.

Example 2: You may have experienced that children make mistakes while counting the numbers. If they attain conservation of order, they would not make mistakes.

Example 3: Pictures showing arrangements of stones in different patterns and the question, "which group has less number of stones?" is asked to children.

I	II	III	IV
0	0000	0	0000000
000	0000	000	000000
00000	0000	0000	
000	0	00000	
0			

If the children could say that each group has the same number, we can conclude that they have developed the power of conservation of the number. Those who do not acquire the power of conservation are unable to understand the difference in size, order, and number. By conservation Piaget means, the ability to pay attention to all details of things and situations and to receive them correctly.

Decentration

While teaching, one might have to pay attention to different aspects of teaching at the same time. These aspects can include description, demonstration and paying attention to each pupil at the same time. One may not have difficulty in doing so. But young children cannot give attention to more than one factor till decentration ability develops.

A child with this ability can classify animals as dogs, cats, cows, etc. but a child having the decentration ability can do more in this regard. S/he could make sub classification such as black dogs, white dogs, red dogs, spotted dogs and so on. This type of classification could be done only by considering more than one factor at a time. The child will be able to consider both shapes and colour at a time. S/he may also be able to consider many characteristics such as shape, size, colour and weight at the same time and so on.

Thus according to Piaget, decentration refers to the ability to consider more than one factor at the same time.

Cognitive Structures

It is easy to understand from our experience that children at different age show difference in mental abilities. Each age group possesses particular mental abilities for that group. Let us see an example.

Raju, a three year old child says that, "the sun comes with me wherever I go. Last week I went to my uncle's house, the sun came and returned with me." The mental ability of this child is suitable to understand the concept of seeing the sun every where only in this fashion. But as the child grows and develops s/he will learn that the sun is not moving with us. The mental abilities of the child help her/him to understand a concept. These mental abilities are referred to as **cognitive structures** by Piaget.

Mental Operations

We are not able to breathe under water, Why? One might put forth the reason to answer the question. Whenever we are exploring reasons, we perform mental operations. Each reasoning process can be done using cognitive structures, which we have seen in the sub section 1.2.5. If we say it more specifically, behind every action there would be mental operations.

Why does one take a chalk piece while going to teach? It may be the same necessity which compels one to take an umbrella when one goes out on a cloudy day. Thus as Piaget defined, mental operations are cognitive structures in action.

These mental operations can be in two ways.

(i) Finding out the reasons and relations as concrete things are manipulated. This is known as Concrete operations.

(ii) Reasoning out and relating in an abstract or hypothetical manner. No concrete objects are necessary to guide the thinking processes here. This is known as formal operations.

Schema

We have already seen that mental structures are responsible for learning. Each new piece of information is internalised as a mental structure. As more information has to be internalised, the more amount of mental structures are required. Each of such mental structure is called a schema. Take the above example of child seeing the elephant for the first time and finally form a concept about it. The development of the required schema or mental structure helps the child to make the concept of elephant. It is developed by the cognitive processes such as conservation and decentration.

Schemes

We have to do various kinds of activities in our daily life. Many of them are routine activities such as brushing, dressing, teaching and so on. Each of such activities could be performed by the working of several mental operations in a series.For instance, teaching includes taking necessary materials, walking to the classroom, writing, drawing, questioning, describing and dictating. All these activities come together in a specific series or pattern to the organisation of your teaching. Similar to teaching, we are performing many of such organised behaviours. This type of organized pattern of behaviour is called a scheme by Piaget. Such schemes help the child in solving various problems in life.

Four Stages of Cognitive Development

According to Piaget, the four stages of cognitive development are sensori-motor period, pre operational period, period of concrete operations and period of formal operations.

Sensori-Motor Period

Children of age up to two years belong to sensori-motor period. Physical activities are the most striking feature of this stage. This stage is very important in the sense that the infant develops basic understanding of her/his surroundings at this stage. The child at this stage develops through the interaction with the physical world. Sucking is a common activity of infants, whatever objects s/he gets, therefore, will be put into her/his mouth.

In this activity the children use mouth for assimilation and accommodation. That is for familiarisation and adjusting with the reality. When they get a new object, disequilibrium occurs and the child tries to restore equilibrium by familiarising the object. Her/his total body is used for this familiarising activity. Towards the end of this stage the child gradually acquires a lot of schemes with regard to many objects by familiarising with them.

The progressive development at this stage leads children to pre operational stage.

Pre Operational Period

Children in the age group of 2-7 years come under this period. The notable features of two year old child is the development of language. The children learn to speak many words by imitating us. And they would be able to use language easily by the completion of development of this stage. Children at this stage ask questions about everything they see. The notable question at this stage is "What is that"? One gets the questions in a series if one answers each of the query. Instead of answering the questions, if someone scold the child, s/he gets very much annoyed.

Another peculiar feature at this stage is the development of the ability to use symbols. We know that children at this stage get engaged in symbolic playing to a certain extent. For example, the famous form of such play is that a group of children symbolically makes a doll house, the bigger ones acting as father and mother. Small piece of wood or a doll is supposed to be a small baby in the house. Using leaves and flowers they prepare food and so on. This beautiful, symbolic play helps them to play their adult role while they grow up into adulthood. The language development at this stage also proceeds through assimilation, accommodation and equilibration. The ability for conservation and decentration also develops. Hence, the schemes on the objects developed earlier get modified and become more accurate. Cognitive structures expand due to new assimilations and accommodation to develop appropriate schemes, so as to result in concept formation.

After the completion of development, the child will proceed to the concrete operational period.

Concrete Operational Period

Children of age group 7 to 11 years belong to this period, the period of concrete operations. Let us try to recognise the markable features of children at this stage. The child is able to do many things 'in head'. That is, s/he is able to think logically. But thinking will be confined to the things and objects familiar to them.

For example, child can be able to select odd one from a group.

1. Squirrel, penguin, languor, lion, sheep
2. Cow, cat, rabbit, goat, buffalo
3. Dog, cat, cow, deer, sheep

Here s/he performs certain mental operations to identify which one is not belonging to group.

S/he is also able to arrange items in serial order. See the following example, Arrange the following words in alphabetical order. Mumbai, Abudhabi, Calicut, Delhi, Kolkata, Ajmer, Chennai, Coimbatore.

The important thing is that, the child needs familiarisation or manipulation of object or activities even at this stage. That is disequilibrium continues and the child assimilates new information, accommodates it and sets equilibrium with the help of visible concrete objects only. Mental operations develop more with the progress in concrete thinking.

Formal Operational Period

Most of the children acquire the skill of formal operations at the age group of 11 to 15 years. There may be transitional period between concrete operations period and formal operations period. Let us see the characteristics of pupils at formal operations stage.

They are able to:

- Learn concepts
- Establish relationships
- List out abstract properties

- Express symbolically
- Reason hypothetically
- Verify and review his own reasoning.

These are some of the major characteristics of pupils at formal operations stage.

Familiarisation still continues as unfamiliar situations and objects are common in daily life. But equilibration at this stage is easier as children are able to accommodate more quickly than in earlier stages. Cognitive structures are developing in such a way to acquire schemes suitable for abstract thinking.

Cognitive Development — Implications to Class Room Learning

Cognitive development has many implications, both inside and outside the class room. In a secondary level classroom, the students might be at the 12+ age group. Theoretically they are at the formal operations stage. But many of them may be at concrete operations stage and at transitional stage. So teaching programme should be designed to cater to the needs of the children at these different stages of cognitive development. Special emphasis should also be given to those who are at the transitional stage. Teacher should provide as many experiences and activities in the class room in order to help them acquire the formal operations ability (more details of teaching shall follow later).

Vygotsky's Postulates on Learner and Learning

Vygotsky's work offers pedagogic approaches to teachers that build on what students know already and support them through dialogue to acquire new knowledge.

Key Elements of Vygotsky's ideas

- Language as the key in learning.
- Children's play – to stimulate cognitive development apart from physical and emotional needs.
- Zone of proximal (potential) development – child can acquire more than what they achieved in tests (as it is performance without assistance) with the help of a more knowledgeable person, here it is a teacher.
- Transferability of thinking process form one context to other – higher order skills such as classifying and logical thinking are transferable.

Implications of Vygotsky's ideas to teaching

- Starting from what children know already and provide them guidance to progress further.

- Teachers using knowledge of how children learn, help them to develop their own thinking on teaching and learning.
- Exploring how children learn rather than what is learned.
- Stimulating classroom discussion so that students can test and verify their learning in collaboration with others.

Language and Children according to Vygotsky

- During the age of 3-7, children think loud when doing tasks and manipulating numbers.
- They increasingly use speech to plan and control their behaviour. Speech developed in relation with their own actions and purposes.
- Seven years onwards speech is related to thinking and planning and started using internal (mental processes) manipulation.

Unique Contribution of Schools and Teachers according to Vygotsky

Vygotsky emphasised the specific roles that schools and teachers play in the cognitive development of children. In contrast to everyday experience, in which children become familiar with the people and objects around them in an unstructured way, Vygotsky explained that school instruction focuses children's minds on structured thinking processes. He referred to this process as the acquisition of 'scientific' concepts. Vygotsky suggested that when children construct meaning they learn to relate causes and effects. Because their experiences in everyday life are not subjected to this construction process, but children think about these experiences in a different way. Vygotsky suggested that the thinking processes which developed in the child at school were instrumental in enabling the child to make more sense of their experiences in life outside school.

Unlike Piaget, who sought to explore children's abilities to form concepts entirely as a result of their own thinking, i.e. in the absence of social interaction ('spontaneous concept' formation), Vygotsky was interested in concepts which developed in the child as a result of teaching at school or from the influence of adults ('non spontaneous' concepts). Piaget believed that concepts learned from teaching at school reflected the adult thinking that the child had learned rather than the child's own thinking, whereas Vygotsky believed that the child not only imitated but reworked the concepts s/he received in order to understand and learn them.

Plan for Teaching based on Vygotsky's Work

From evidences drawn from clinical studies, Vygotsky put forth a number of propositions about learning in children. Although many of his ideas were based on interactions between an adult and a single child, Vygotsky nonetheless regarded each child as a member of a social environment.

His suggestions included the following: children's achievement when assisted by an adult, tells us more about their capacity to learn than in IQ tests; learning of a concept, word or phrase, etc, is followed by a longer process of the child's development of thinking, that includes learning when and how it can be used. Recognising when it is being used by somebody else, using and learning how to use it in conjunction with reasoning processes (to make deductions, to interpret, to relate causes and effects, etc.). Effective teaching is that which not only builds on what a child understands already, but that is a stimulus to a new series of thinking processes in the child. In this context, assessment of learning is highly significant. It enables teachers to identify and use what pupils know already to plan their teaching.

Individual Constructivists' Views on Learning

One strand of constructivism has its origin in Piaget's genetic epistemology and related cognitive science views. The notion that intelligence organises the world by organising itself reflects that Piaget's central concern was with the process by which humans construct their knowledge of the world. Piaget postulated the existence of cognitive schemes that are formed and developed through the coordination and internalisation of a person's actions on realities in the world. These schemes evolve as a result of equilibration, a process of adaptation to more complex experiences. New schemes thus come into being and modifying the old ones.

According to this individual constructionist's view, meaning is made by individuals and depends on the individual's current knowledge schemes. Therefore, learning occurs when those schemes are changed by the resolution of disequilibration. Such resolution requires internal mental activity and results in development of new knowledge scheme.

In essence, understanding means constructing and modifying knowledge schemes in students' minds. Understanding goes beyond knowing. It requires learners' dynamic mental activities.

Social Constructivists' Views on Learning

While individual constructivism places primary importance on seeing meaning-making as a cognitive process in the individual, the social constructivism focuses on an account of individuals, as they function in social contexts. A social constructivist perspective recognises that learning involves being introduced to a specific cultural community. Bruner (1985) introduced Vygotsky's work to express this perspective.

In this perspective, knowledge and its understanding are constructed when individuals engage socially in talk and activity about shared problems and tasks. Making meaning is thus a dialogic process, involving persons in conversations, and learning is seen as the process by which individuals are introduced to a culture by more skilled members. So learning makes learners appropriate cultural tools through their involvement in the activities of this culture. Throughout the learning process, a more experienced member of a culture supports a less experienced member by structuring tasks.

In sum, in social constructivists' view, meaning-making is portrayed as originating in social interactions between individuals, or as individuals' interactions with cultural products that are made available to them in books or other sources. (Leach & Scott, 2003)

Paradigm Shift in Science Learning — Individual Constructivists' Views to Social Constructivists' Views

According to Piagetian perspective, learning science is seen as involving a process of conceptual change. Consequently, social constructivists assert that to construct knowledge beyond personal empirical inquiry, learners should be given access to the knowledge system of science, that is, the concepts and models of conventional science. Social constructivists agree that insights about students' 'mental structures' are useful in explaining why science is difficult to learn for many students. Consideration of the social environment through which students learn scientific ideas is necessary.

In addition, in a social constructivists' perspective the intended products of science learning (i.e., science concepts) are cultural. Concepts cannot generally be perceived by individuals, they are validated through complex empirical and social processes, and are used within scientific communities for particular purposes. Therefore, scientific knowledge can only be learned through some process of social transmission. (Leach & Scott, 2003)

In social constructivists' view, moreover, given the situation with so many students in a classroom, teachers can hardly plan instructions to address each student's momentary and individual development. Therefore, much consideration should be given on, how the knowledge to be taught is introduced in the social environment of the classroom, and how individual students become able to use that knowledge for themselves. (Driver et al, 1994; Leach & Scott, 2003)

Summing Up

We have discussed the basic aspects of cognitive development. The knowledge of the developmental stage of the learners would help the teacher to improve teaching.

i) The basic concepts of cognitive development put forth by Piaget such as adaptation, equilibration, conservation, decentration, cognitive structures mental operations, schema and schemes.
ii) The four stages of cognitive development are sensori-motor period, pre operational period, period of concrete operations and period of formal operations.
iii) There are implications for this theory in various aspects of teaching such as instructional process, nature of examples, nature of experience, etc.
iv) Basic postulates of Vygotsky on learner and learning, and different aspects of individual and social constructivism on teaching and learning.

Chapter 2
Learner's Characteristics

Important Characteristics of Learners at Secondary Level

Each stage of mental development has its own peculiar characteristics. The progressive changes in mental development reach its completion at the end of the teenage. We have to brush up the characteristics of their developmental stage. So let us try to identify the characteristics of pupils at the concrete operational stage.

Identification of Children at Concrete Operational Stage

Development at this stage begins at the age of seven and goes up to almost till the age of eleven years. Let us see an example to understand the nature of students at this level.

A group of fourth standard students are playing in a garden. There are two huge May flower trees with red flowers. One of these children said,

> "This tree is flowering as a memento for our summer vacation, what is its name?"
> "May flower," said someone.
> "Why is it called so?"
> "It is because the month in which it flowers."
> "Why do they have red flowers?" The group is thrown into confusion for a moment. After a little thought one said,
> "It is because of the strong sunlight and heat. Don't you know the metal turn red in the blacksmith's workshop? Surely it is same as that."
> "That is true," the group got an answer to solve their confusion.

The children at this stage would be able to reason out, but the reasoning is related to objects as we see/familiar as in the earlier example. The physical world and the manipulation of objects alone come to the thinking and reasoning of children at this stage. They are able to make observation and draw inference. But they are not able to consider all possibilities as we see in the example. They are also able to identify phenomenon but it will be unsystematic and incomplete. Though they are able to identify the flowering phenomenon but they are unaware of the other aspects of flowering.

Identification of Children at Formal Operational Stage

Formal operation thoughts are the characteristic feature of the age group of 11-15 years. So, the pupils at secondary level belong to this category.

Let us examine a group of secondary school students beneath the same May flower trees. The discussion of the group can be as follows.

"How beautiful these flowers are!"
"Why do they flower at this particular time of the year?"
"Hormones are responsible for that. Atmospheric conditions influence activation of hormones."
"Why do they have red colour?"
"Because they reflect red colour only."

As in the example they are able to reason out concepts, express relationships, and they can express their thoughts in symbolic terms.

The cognitive development takes its final form at the end of this stage and the difference with adults is in respect to the depth of experience only. Children will be less experienced than adults.

Unique Characteristics of Secondary Level Pupils — Early Adolescence

The age of this group ranges from 12 to 14 years, but pupils above 14 years also are common in our schools. As we have seen in the sub section (2.2.2) they belong to the formal operational stage. So mentally they are able to perform the highest level of thought. They have lack of experience, so we have to provide more and more examples while teaching, to enrich their experience.

The physical and biological characteristics of the pupils at this stage are given in this section. The unique characteristics of secondary level pupils are those of early adolescence. So, let us have a discussion on various aspects of adolescence to realise the peculiarities at this stage.

Meaning of Adolescence

Adolescence is a transitional stage in every person's life in which s/he has lost her/his childhood. This is said to be the "period of storm and stress". The hormonal secretions, sudden biological growth and appearance of secondary sexual characteristics increase stress in pupils at this stage. As high school teachers, you are familiar with adolescents.

Important Characteristics of Adolescents

A child knows her/his role clearly, an adult also knows the role very well, but an adolescent is in role-confusion. Let us see the example of Suresh, a fourteen year old boy. He was a problem child for all teachers, when one of the teachers enquired about his family and his personal life, he broke down. On the one hand parents considered him as too young, and on the other they scolded him for not behaving like a grown-up man because he is as big as his father in appearance. This role-confusion leads him to aggressive behaviour. Effective counselling can help to channelise him into right way and then he can become one of the best students in the school.

Two major characteristics of adolescents such as *role-confusion*, i.e. the confusion as to how to behave in a situation, and *openness of adolescents* are clear through this example.

At the time of counselling, Suresh said that actually he has respect for teachers, but the need for getting attention from others made him mischievous in the classroom. He also wanted to exhibit his independent role. The counselling helped him to strive for the need for achievement, by which he succeeded very well.

Though adolescents are in role-confusion, they have *need for getting attention, need for independence, and need for achievement.*

Biju and Raju are classmates. Mujeeb, Thomas and Shiju are in close company with them. They have common interest, dressing, hair style, etc. So they form a group — peer groups are very common among adolescents. Each member in a peer group has great concern and intimacy with other members of the group. They consider the opinions of their group members' valuable than those of adults. So forming peer group is another characteristic of adolescents.

Biological growth, appearance of secondary sexual characteristics, and sexual maturity are the other marked characteristics of adolescence. All these push adolescents into extreme sensitivity, adjustment problems and insecurity.

Since adolescent have peculiar characteristics, specific educational programmes are necessary to meet the needs of adolescents.

Effective Dealing of Adolescents

Jose, a secondary school teacher, is experienced in dealing with adolescents very effectively. Let us see, what he is doing in the classroom.

Among the group of students he appeared like a group member, guide and sometimes as an elder brother. He usually uses group investigation and discussion methods for instruction. He tries to give more responsibilities to students, give opportunities for self expression and create an atmosphere that everyone is at the centre of attraction. Grouping of students also is done within the classroom for group works. This grouping is done on the basis of peer group in which each student belongs. From own experience he said that counselling is the best way for dealing with adolescents effectively and praising is highly influential than punishment.

While analysing the above example, we could infer some important points in dealing with adolescents. Many problems that adolescents face are new to them. So, ways should be searched to help them in resolving their worries, clearing their doubts, sharing experiences, and in satisfying their needs. Special efforts are to be made to give them responsibilities and freedom. Necessary guidance should be given to them and if necessary, to their parents also.

Exceptional Children

Who are Exceptional Children?

The exceptional child is a child who deviates from average or normal child. This include gifted children, backward children, mentally retarded, mentally ill, learning disabled, physical difference in abilities, hearing or visual impairment and multiple differential abilities. *Gifted children* are those who have high mental abilities. *Backward children* are those who are not able to achieve as per their abilities.

- *Mentally retarded children* are those having low mental abilities.
- *Learning disabled* are those who have certain disabilities in learning.
- *Multiple differential abilities* are those with more than one physical disabilities.

Gifted Children — Characteristics

Let us see how gifted children deviate from the normal children.

a) They show high interest in reading at an age before six years.
b) They also participate in extra-curricular activities much more than average students.
c) Most of them have interest to take professional occupation in their future life.

You might have experienced a number of gifted students in your career. It is very essential to identify the gifted students in classroom, which helps you to organise peer teaching. Usually you can employ intelligence tests and rating scales to identify giftedness. Let us examine the necessary programme for the education of the gifted children.

Education of Gifted Children: Gifted students usually need some additional works. If they do not get additional activities, they will definitely be a headache. So it is essential to develop a special programme for the gifted students.

This programme should include problem solving, discovery learning, individual techniques for learning and peer teaching.The teacher should use additional activities and problems solving to the gifted students. The teacher should plan in advance to develop problems for gifted ones concerned with each lesson / chapter. For example, use the following problems for the chapter 'our environment'.

a) "The absence of one trophic level affects the equilibrium in an ecosystem" Critically examine the statement with the aid of supplementary data.
b) Construction of still models of food chain, energy flow, and biological pyramids.

Activities like this would help them to cater to their interest in learning.

Peer teaching is another activity which helps to deal effectively with the gifted students. Utilise them to the benefit of their classmates through peer teaching. Necessary guidance should be given to them before the conduct of peer teaching.

Backward Children

Backward children are backward in academic achievement. There are variety of backward children.

Backward students are unable to achieve up to the level which is expected from them, based on their level of intelligence. The causes of backwardness in students are as follows:

1) Emotional factors such as anxiety, tension and depression.
2) Unproductive home environment
3) Lack of interest of students.
4) Factors concerning school such as unsuitable method of teaching, inadequate learning activities, and insufficient accessory learning materials.

Identification of Backward Children: Achievement test is the easiest tool to identify backward children. Especially teacher should measure achievement in language, arithmetic and general knowledge. If achievement of a child does not reach up to the expected level, then s/he will be a backward child. Assessing the level of intelligence of the child and predicting the possible level of achievement is a more scientific method for locating backwardness.

Observational rating scales, cumulative records and case study are other effective tools to identify backward children.

Dealing with Backward children: As the children have no mental disability, the teacher could guide them to at least average level of achievement. The following points will help you in this regard.

i) Encouraging backward children — simple encouraging comments such as 'good' you have done it well 'well done', etc. will be very effective.
ii) Adopting suitable method of teaching — one of the causes of backwardness is lack of interest. Methods of teaching which stimulate and sustain interest in students should be tried.
iii) Learning by doing — more opportunity to the backward children to participate in learning activities should be provided.

These are the various procedures which help in dealing effectively with backward children. There is a category of children with more serious problem, i.e. learning disabilities and is discussed here under.

Learning Disabilities

In every classroom there can be at least one child who fails to keep up with other students in academic achievement. Such students might have learning disabilities and these can be of different types.

What is Learning Disability?

Learning disability may be exhibited as a disorder in one or more basic psychological process involved in understanding or using spoken or written language. These may lead to disorder of listening, talking, reading, and writing. Learning problems due to visual, hearing, motor handicaps, and mental retardation do not come under learning disabilities. So learning disability may have occurred due to perceptual handicaps or brain injury.

Perceptual handicap means inability in perception, e.g., a child with perceptual handicap could not perceive a written page as such. The child could not perceive even sentences or words, but only letters. Brain injury means injury and damage to brain cells before or after birth due to various reasons. The brain injured children might have normal intelligence. But they have learning problems due to their perceptual, conceptual or behavioural difficulties, which cause lower achievement.

Certain children with learning disability may show distractibility, hyper activity and lack of perseverance. Here, distractibility means inability to concentrate on a subject. Hyperactivity is purposeless, uncontrollable activities, shown by disabled children. And perseverance is the ability to focus attention on a given task, until it is completed. So in essence, learning disability is inability in understanding and using or performing various activities related to learning. For example, while listening music, one would have listened to its rhythm, words, back ground voice modulation, etc. One can recite it once or twice you have exposed to the music. But a child with learning disability could not listen to music as you do, and could not receive the music also.

Dealing with Learning Disabled Children: It is not an easy task to deal effectively with learning disabled children, because each one of them has unique problem in learning. The first step you should do is to identify the children with learning disabilities. The identification should be done at an early stage of life. Then only, you could develop suitable plan for proper development of children with learning disabilities.

Examining the learning activities of children and the mistakes made by them will help you locate children with learning disability. Along with this specially designed tools are also helpful to identify the disability and its extent. Once you have identified the children with learning disabilities, you should adopt suitable educational programmes for their benefit. It is better to give them instructions with the help of neurologists in the beginning, using appropriate methods, and by parental involvement. Such education will help the disabled children to overcome their difficulty to a greater extent. So in short, the time of detection of learning disability has crucial role in overcoming such difficulties.

CHAPTER 3
Teaching the Learner

As we have to teach the learners, we should know the details of learners, their needs and appropriate teaching strategies.

Needs of the Learner

The needs of the learner can be categorised into three categories: on the basis of cognitive level; needs on the basis of learning abilities; and special needs. Analysis of such needs would help to chalk out suitable strategies of instruction.

Needs on the Basis of Cognitive Level: We have already discussed the characteristics of secondary school pupils. So, you are familiar with identifying learners belonging to particular cognitive level. You will say that, learners at the secondary stage belong to twelve plus age group. So, naturally they will be either at the end of concrete operations stage or at the beginning of the formal operations stage. More specifically, majority of them may be at transitional stage between the two. So children at this stage need special help from you to apply formal operations correctly. They have to get enough experience to perform formal operations. They also need help in problem solving. So you should provide as many situations as possible for applying formal operations correctly. Thus, the need of bridging the gap between these two stages is the major need of children at this stage.

They also have a need for continuous opportunities to interact with the environment. Unfamiliar situations and examples should puzzle the children at this stage and tempt them to act as in the previous stage of cognitive development. The students at this stage should be properly motivated, and then only they may try to solve newer problems using newer methods.

Needs on the Basis of Learning Abilities: We have already discussed about children with varied levels of learning abilities, and know that each one has her/his own needs on the basis of the learning abilities. It could be that the majority of students in our classrooms might be of average ability — some of them may have special abilities and some others may have certain disabilities.

Let us first consider the needs of children with special abilities, namely the gifted and talented children. The prime need of the gifted students is need for identification of their talents. If they do not get proper identification, they may become problem children. Take the case of Basheer, a tenth standard student. He is the student having high IQ and special interest in electrical and electronics. When he was admitted to eighth standard he could not get any recognition for his talents. Soon he became a problem child, who lost his interest in studies and start disturbing the classroom. His science teacher praised him for his performance at the upper primary stage, and enquired about his area of interests and hobbies. By the end of that conversation, Basheer was able to regain his self confidence with the help of the science teacher. He developed and exhibited a project on electronics in the national science exhibition. He started showing high interest in reading also. This shows that when one gets proper recognition and proper environment, s/he could regain the level of academic achievement. So, the need of identification of abilities and the proper environment for development are the two major needs of the gifted students.

In the case of backward children also identification is one of the basic needs. Nobody is willing to consider himself as backward in any respect. So, a student with hearing disability will try to conceal his disability and sit among other students. They also may have a feeling of insecurity because of the reason of their backwardness. So need for emotional security and need for self confidence are the basic needs of disabled students. A need for special attention will be there in them, though, they wish for that, they would not try to demand it openly. Therefore, we should be vigilant on the identification of children with special abilities and inabilities, along with average children and their needs.

Special Needs: The students at secondary level belong to 12 plus group. This group is otherwise called as teen age and psychologically as adolescence. As discussed that they have special nature, they also have special needs. Let us see what their special needs are. The peer group is a milestone in the social development of children, naturally there occur an intense desire for group formation. It can be inferred as a need for socialisation. Adolescence is a period of emotional insecurity also. So there of course is need for emotional integrity. So it is your duty to safeguard the needs of adolescents.

We all are very eager to establish our self-identify, likewise the adolescents also have a need for recognition. Some of them get it through academic achievement. Some others gained it through their achievement in sports, games and other curricular activities. Yet others try to be known through students' organisations. Some others get recognition as they are big or small physically. They might become problem children to establish their identity. So we could infer that the need for recognition is very strong in adolescents.

Selecting Suitable Teaching Strategies

Whatever we plan is meant for improving the instruction. We usually have to adopt a variety of teaching strategies. The selection of a particular strategy is on the basis of certain aspects. Strategy means a preplanned set of activities, arranged in logical order to achieve a desired end. The important aspects in the selection of teaching strategies are as under.

Basis for Selection of Teaching Srategy

Since, a teaching strategy is meant to teach a particular part of the topic, you have to utilise more than one strategy to teach a single topic. The following are the bases for selection of teaching strategies:

1. *Level of learners*: This is one of the aspects which helps to determine the teaching strategy. Teacher has to consider the cognitive level of the learners, s/he cannot adopt the same strategy for students in different standards. The strategy used should be helpful to develop formal operations of students. The exercise given at this stage should be helpful to improve formal reasoning abilities. For example, the following exercise can be given in the chapter 'Environment: make a study on the impact of pollution on environment'.
2. *Difficulty level of the topic*: Teacher may be able to teach two different topics using the same teaching strategy, if they are not different in difficulty level. Say for example, the introductory lesson on environment could be developed using question answer and discussion strategies. A lesson on the lethal effect of pollution could be taught experimentally and using survey methods.
3. *Needs of the learner*: The gifted and backward children have difference in needs. Needs of the gifted children are far different from that of the backward ones. So teacher has to select and use strategies which are capable of satisfying the needs of the learners. For example, using peer teaching to cater the needs of the gifted and the backward ones. Additional exercises should be given to the gifted students and supplementary works should be given to the backward ones.

UNIT 2

Planning for Teaching Science at Secondary Level

CHAPTER 4

Long Term Planning and Unit Planning

For the success of any endeavour planning is necessary; education being no exception. Planning in education can be at different levels.

United Nations, through Millennium Development Goals, created a platform for 'Education for All' at international level. There can be broad educational planning for the whole nation and then for each state. There can be planning for the primary, secondary and tertiary levels of education. Each level of education is given through different institutions. Each institution has its own planning. Both long term planning and short term planning will be done in every institution at appropriate time. One of the major types of planning is planning for teaching. Teaching plan also has different levels. Planning can be for more than one year: for an academic year; for a term; and for a unit. Such planning helps in better management of teaching.

LONG TERM PLANNING

Long Term planning includes careful and purposive work of teaching. Let us see the important aspects of long term planning.

Meaning

We use long term planning to refer to the process of planning for an academic year or for more than one year. The duration of the plan is not so important. But aspects included and the nature of work done, are significant. Group of teachers of the same subject in an institution sit together and prepare the plan for the given period of time is done in long term planning. Now we shall discuss the components of a long term plan.

Components of a Long term Plan

The major components of a long term plan are number of teachers, number of standards and divisions, levels of teaching, units in each standard, time allotted to each standard, instructional strategies, accessory learning materials, scheme of evaluation, grading and promotion, and co-curricular activities. Let us see these components in detail.

Number of teachers: The total number of teachers in each subject in a particular institution is a major component of long term plan. This is because the work is divided among all the teachers of a subject. So the number of teachers available is directly proportional to the work load of each teacher.

Number of standards and divisions: The number of students in each division and the number of division for each *standard* in the institution are the second component of long term plan. The difficulty in teaching increases with the increase in the strength of students.

Levels of teaching: The level of teaching such as primary, upper primary, secondary and higher secondary, if any is the third component of long term plan.

Units in each standard: We all teach on the basis of prescribed syllabus. The syllabus of each standard is divided into different units. The number of units in each standard and difficulty level of units also is an important component of long term plan.

Time allotted for each standard: We are usually teaching English for six periods per week in tenth standard. Likewise, you know all the subjects have period allotment. So the time available for each subject is another component of long term plan.

Instructional strategies: We are practising a variety of instructional strategies such as lecture, discussion, demonstration, experimentation, group investigation, group discussion, project, discovery, etc. Different instructional strategies are needed to teach each unit. So it is essential to identify the appropriate instructional strategy well in advance to facilitate instruction. So it becomes another component of long plan.

Accessory learning materials: Usually we are using different types of materials to facilitate learning. These materials are referred to as accessory learning materials or learning aids. It is essential to identify the necessary learning aids in advance. This would help in collecting or preparing the materials.

Scheme of evaluation: Scheme of evaluation is another component of long term plan. We all know evaluation is the integral part of instruction. So it is very essential for planning for evaluation early enough.

Grading and promotion: The procedure for grading and criteria for promotion become the other components of long term plan. Planning in advance regarding these aspects would reduce the work load at the end of the academic year.

Co-curricular activities: Co-curricular activities such as science fair, science club, excursions and field trips are in close relation with classroom instruction. The schedule of each of such activities should be determined while preparing the long term plan.

Steps in Long Term Planning

In any type of planning, there is planning board which has the right to develop the plan. In long term planning also, the planning will be done by a council of teachers. There are councils in each subject (i.e. Subject Councils).

So the first step in long term planning is the meeting of each subject council separately.

The second step is the preparation of an outline schedule for the long term plan. The structure of the schedule is subjected to thorough discussion before giving its final form. This is the third step.

The discussion on the existing facilities and necessities of the school and finalising the plan are included in the final step of long term planning.

Use of Long Term Planning

Long term planning is meant for a year or more than a year, as it should be helpful in achieving the targeted change and long term objectives. The existing facilities in the institution and shortcoming could be realised by this type of planning. The thrust area requiring attention should also be explored out. The planning at the beginning of an academic year would be helpful to determine the instructional strategies, strategies of evaluation, grading and promotion. This is also useful in the preparation of accessory learning materials and other resources and its proper utilisation. The co-curricular activities such as science fair, field trip, etc. can also be carried out effectively. In short, we could infer that long term planning will be helpful in the better management of instruction and in providing a variety of learning experiences to learners.

A Format of Long term Plan

A format of long term plan will give you the whole picture of the institution regarding, subject, teachers, instructional activities, accessory learning materials, evaluation strategies and co-curricular activities for a year. So, you should use the format of long term plan to plan the activities of your institution for an academic year.

UNIT PLANNING

In long term planning, we could identify the difficulty level of units, instructional strategies to be adopted and necessary learning aids needed for instruction of each unit. It was a sort of generalised planning. Let us see the meaning of unit planning.

Meaning

Learning materials are arranged as units. There may be a number of units of instruction in a given science course. The units as in Xth standard biology are nervous co-ordination, sense organs, chemical co-ordination, environment, etc. Teaching the content as units as a whole have more instructional value, otherwise each lesson should be conceived as unrelated facts. Unit planning is a detailed plan of selected materials organised for effective instruction for a particular class. The plan you make for teaching the unit, sense organs in standard ten is an example for unit planning for teaching that unit. In short, unit planning involves planning of all processes of classroom instruction for a given unit.

Components of a Unit Plan

You have enormous experience in lesson planning. But in usual teaching profession the scope of unit planning seems to be neglected. A good unit plan should have the following components:

Introduction	The introductory part involves the name of unit, grade level of students, time needed to cover up the unit and the time of commencement
Statement of objectives	The objectives to be realised by the completion of the unit must be stated in behavioural terms. These include specific understanding, skills and attitudes. The details of stating objectives are discussed in first chapter of Unit 6.
Outline of content	This component involves important concepts in the unit, problems to be solved, subject matter heading and projects to be completed.
Learning activities	A list of learning activities to achieve the pre-stated objectives should be prepared next. The approximate time required for each activity should be mentioned along with the sequential arrangement of such activities.
Resources and materials	The next component of unit plan is the resources and materials needed for the instruction of particular unit. These include printed materials, audio visual aids, list of consultants available in the community, and an outline of the necessary procedure to facilitate the use-of-out of class resources.
Evaluation procedure	This is final component of a unit plan. This includes a list of evaluation procedures to determine student's development and achievement of specific objectives for the unit, such as quiz, unit test, summaries, home assignment written and oral reports and pupils projects.

Structure of Unit Plan

We shall see here an outline of a unit plan. A model unit plan is also given.

Unit Heading

i. Objectives of the unit
ii. Previous knowledge
iii. Major problems / issues
iv. Content outline
v. Concepts/skills to be developed
vi. Vocabulary
vii. Possible experiments / demonstrations/activities
viii. Possible discussion topics
ix. Audio-visual materials
x. Areas need further enrichment
xi. Teachers' Bibliography
xii. Students' Bibliography
xiii. Scheme for evaluation

This is a proposed outline for a unit. A model unit plan developed as per this outline is given in the next section.

Model Unit Plan

Model unit on 'Our Environment' will help to develop unit plan of the choice.

UNIT — OUR ENVIRONMENT

Standard: X
Time required: 10 Hrs.
Time of commencement: October third week

I. Objectives

1. interpret scientific facts
2. analyse relationship between the relevant facts
3. develop an awareness about the means of conservation of our environment
4. develop positive attitude towards population control
5. develop positive attitude against pollution
6. develop scientific appreciation

II. Previous Knowledge

(i) knowledge of animal adaptation
(ii) knowledge of food habits of organisms
(iii) knowledge of elements needed for plant growth
(iv) knowledge about population growth and over population
(v) knowledge about basic aspects of pollution

III. Major problems

- What is the use of solar energy in an ecosystem?
- What are the components in a food chain?
- Why does energy flow from one level to the other?
- Why are Bio-geo chemical cycles important for living beings?
- How does human involvement disturb ecological balance?
- What are the lethal effects of pollution?

IV. Content outline

Biosphere – sun, source of energy – green plants, Herbivores, Carnivores – Autotrophy and Heterotrophy – food chain and food web – Energy flow – Bio- geo chemical cycles – Equilibrium in Eco system – Human involvement in ecosystem – Pollution.

V. Concepts to be developed

1. Ecology is study of animals and its relationship with environment
2. Ecosystem is composed of biotic and abiotic components
3. Food web is an inter connection of different trophic levels
4. The flow of energy is unidirectional
5. Bio-geo chemical cycles are essential for existence of nature
6. Human involvement leads to ecological imbalances
7. Pollution is harmful to living beings

VI. Vocabulary

The vocabulary should be grouped as A, B, C, etc. according to the order of sub sections in the unit.

A	B	C
Community	Autotrophy	Producer
Ecosystem	Heterotrophy	Consumer
Bioshpere	Trophic level	Decomposer
	Food chain	Saprophyte
	Food web	
D	**E**	**F**
Energy flow	Bio-geo chemical cycles	Acid rain
Energy ladder	Carbon Cycle	Aerosol spray propellants
Pyramid of numbers	Oxygen cycle	Pollution
Pyramid of biomass	Water cycle	
	Nitrogen cycle	

VII. Possible experiments / demonstrations / activities

1. Survey of living beings in an ecosystem and construct;
   (a) food chain
   (b) food web
   (c) Pyramid of numbers and
   (d) Pyramid of biomass
2. Make a list of human involvement leading to ecological imbalances in your locality
3. Survey of pollution at your locality.

VIII. Possible Discussion Topics

1. Importance of solar energy
2. Relevance of each trophic level in maintaining ecological balance
3. Necessity of elements to be cycled in nature
4. Hazards of ecological imbalances
5. Lethal effects of pollution.

IX. Audio Visual Materials

1. Charts of food chain, food web, energy flow, pyramid of numbers, pyramid of biomass, Bio-geo chemical cycles
2. Models of Bio-geo chemical cycles and energy ladder
3. Films on nature, and pollution

X. Areas need further enrichment

1. Ecological problems in Kerala
2. Pollution — a worldwide problem
3. Nature of human involvement leading to destruction of ecosystem

XI. Teachers' Bibliography

1) Odoum, E.P. - Ecology
2) Verma - Environmental biology

XII. Students' Bibliography

1. Science magazines
2. Science articles
3. Science programmes on various TV channels

XIII. Scheme for Evaluation

- Home assignment
- Quiz
- Students project

- a) Survey on an ecosystem
    1. Survey to realise causes of pollution
- Unit test

This is a model unit plan for the teaching unit 'Our Environment'.

Summing Up

This chapter has discussed the important aspects of long term planning and unit planning. The structural aspects had have been given more importance. The main points are:

a) Long term planning involves the planning of teaching for an year or more, involving aspects such as teachers, students, levels of teaching, teaching units, time allotted at each standard, instructional strategies, accessory learning materials, scheme of evaluation, grading and promotion and co-curricular activities.

b) Long term planning must be done in each subject separately.

c) Long term planning would help in achieving the targeted change.

d) A unit plan is planning of teaching a unit which includes components such as introduction, objectives, content outline, learning activities, resource materials and evaluation procedures.

e) The illustrative model unit plan acts as an outline for unit developers.

Chapter 5

Lesson Planning

Thorough planning is essential for effective instruction. The science teacher should select and organise suitable methods and materials for classroom instruction. Usually, the contents of a chapter are divided as different lessons. So it is essential to plan for each lesson for effective instruction. The format of lesson plan has less importance. But the originality in thinking and the efficiency in planning by the teacher have more importance, as it directs her/him to identify most effective procedures for achieving the aims and objectives of the lesson.

Meaning

Syllabus for any class consists of several chapters. Each of such chapter needs several hours of instruction based on the nature and complexity of the topic. Lesson plan is a plan of activities which will be selected and organised to achieve pre-stated objectives within the contents of a lesson. Somc of our teachers have lesson plan in their mind, while they are going to teach. But the constant advancements in science and science content make it necessary to revise the plan year after year in a detailed manner so as to incorporate new inventions in the field. Most of the educationists are of the view that daily lesson plans are vital to both experienced and beginning teachers in improving their teaching efficiency.

Components of a Lesson Plan

We are familiar with the components of lesson plan. These include the following items such as statement of the topic, objectives, content outline, procedure of instruction and evaluation of the lesson. Let us see these components one by one.

Statement of the topic: Statement of the topic can be done in different ways. It can be as a general heading in the form of a principle, concept or law. For example, the introductory lesson in the unit 'Our Environment', can be stated as in any of the following titles. 'Ecology and Biosphere' or "Ecosystem" or 'Living beings are closely related to nonliving materials' or "An ecosystem consists of all components in harmony".

Objectives of the lesson: The objectives should be at different levels, such as knowledge, understanding, application and skill. Both process and product objectives need to be included. But all categories of objectives will not come under a single lesson. Long range objectives such as scientific attitude must have a place in lesson; it could be realised over a long period of instruction.

Outline of content: The outline of content should act as a guide to the teacher. The nature of content determines the nature of learning activities. The content also is based on objectives. For example, in a lesson on environment, students need to do research, to conduct survey and investigation to understand the problem laid by the lesson. Thus this content helps to realise the objectives. Whatever it is, the content should include all significant concepts of the topic which may influence the life of the learner.

Instructional methods: We are usually practising a number of instructional methods. Among them the lecture method is the dominant one. Lecture method has least scope in teaching science. This happens because many of us do not try to make a list of methods or procedure for teaching our daily lessons. Advance planning would help us to understand which method is suitable to a particular content and to realise the objectives of the lesson.

The following factors are the determinants of appropriate methods. The factors are objectives, content, needs of the learners, personality of teacher and nature of the class. The selection may be for a single method or more from the group of methods such as demonstration, discussion, problem solving, modified problem solving, laboratory, open ended experiments, case study, lecture method, field trip, group investigation, project method, etc.

Procedure for evaluation: Evaluation is the integral part of instruction. Evaluation in the class room will be helpful to determine to what extent learning occurs. Therefore, a variety of methods are used for this purpose. Tests, assignments, seminar, collection, construction, project report, careful observation of students, etc., are useful for evaluation. The written reports as well as oral responses would also act as the source of evaluation. This part is very important, as the amount of learning occurred would have direct role on subsequent learning. An example is that a student who does not know addition will not be able to calculate the cost of two things easily.

Steps in Lesson Planning

Division of lessons from chapter: In first chapter of this unit, a unit plan on the chapter, Our Environment has been discussed. Each of such chapters consists of many lessons. The first step in lesson planning is the breaking down of lessons from a chapter. Taking a lesson from a chapter depends on the length of the content, concepts to be developed, and required learning strategies that should be taken into consideration. The chapter 'Our Environment' may involve lessons such as biosphere, food chain and food web, energy flow, biological pyramids, bio-geo chemical cycles – carbon cycle, nitrogen cycle, water cycle, oxygen cycle, balance in ecosystem and pollution.

Identification of objectives: The second step in lesson planning is determining the scope of the lesson. The scope of lesson in turn helps to determine the objectives of the lesson. The objectives of the lesson would be helpful in determining further steps of lesson planning. The objectives should be stated in simple and clear terms by incorporating content part as well as behavioural part.

Identification of previous knowledge: The learning of new things should be based on the existing ones. That is, learning of anything requires some previous learning. This in turn acts as previous knowledge. For example, for learning a lesson on biosphere, knowledge about adaptations, community life of animals and their inter-relations is necessary.

Determine the content outline: As a first step in lesson planning, we should divide a chapter into its component lessons. In each lesson, the selected content should be arranged as concepts or principles or laws. For example biosphere is composed of living and non-living materials. The content selected should be significant to the level and needs of the learner for the present as well as future.

Selection of instructional methods: The next step is the selection of suitable methods of instruction. Instructional method means procedure adopted for instruction. Instructional methods should be based on the nature of the content of the lesson. For example, the lesson on pollution can be instructed using discussion, problem solving and group investigation methods. Likewise, suitable methods can be selected accordingly for various other lessons.

Determine the nature of learning activities: The nature of content and instructional method determines the nature of learning activities. Learning activities means selected activities used for learning. A variety of learning activities can be involved in a lesson. For example, the instructional method problem solving can include learning activities like observation, discussion, experimentation, verification, etc. The selection of learning activities also depends on the facilities available, personality of teacher and nature of students.

Selection of materials and resources: Teaching of each lesson needs certain accessory learning materials. The number and variety of such materials will depend upon the nature of content, instructional methods and learning activities. For example, a lesson on pollution needs resource materials such as photographs, charts and films. Direct observation and survey also will be useful. So, certain community resources are also necessary for effective instruction on pollution.

Selection of evaluation procedure: The final step of lesson planning is selection of evaluation procedure. Deciding the proper evaluation procedure is essential to determine the degree of learning. Usually learning is evaluated on the basis of the nature and level of pupils' responses. There are many methods of evaluation for classroom learning. It is the teacher, who has the right to select the appropriate procedure with respect to the student and the content.

Lesson Plan — An Illustration

Topic: Balance in Ecosystem Standard - X

Objectives

The pupils will be able to:

1. Recall the meaning of ecosystem, natural resources, exploitation of nature, and equilibrium of nature.
2. Identify the negative effects of over population.
3. Develop positive attitude towards conservation of nature.
4. ....(you can add)

Previous knowledge

- Preliminary knowledge about ecosystem.
- Knowledge about interaction between animals and their surroundings.
- Knowledge about hazards of over-population.
- Knowledge of environmental destruction.

Content outline

The lesson begins with the following statement. *Though we are employing advance technology and fertilisers, the rate of production decreases year after year.*

After analysing this statement the following concepts can be discussed:

1. Living beings in a particular locality maintain equilibrium by means of interaction.
2. Exploitation of nature and natural resources disturb the equilibrium in nature Over-population and technological developments lead to ecological imbalances.

Instructional methods

Group investigation can be the major method along with discussion and lecture methods. Investigation should be guided and directed to understand the concepts well. A field trip has to be conducted to survey the disturbances that have been made by human beings in an ecosystem. The observations can be conducted in the subsequent class periods.

Learning activities

The learning activities including questioning, discussing, observing, analysing and experimenting can be included.

Materials and resources

Accessory learning materials such as charts, news clips, photographs and films can be used.

Community resources such as pond, river and forest also can be used to investigate the nature and causes of ecological imbalances.

Evaluation procedure

Throughout the lesson, the evaluation is to be done by observing the nature of pupil responses. Teacher will give guidance for the investigation and direct the discussion. Meanwhile the teacher will evaluate students' ability to make observations and draw inferences. Analysis of students' opinions during discussion will help to evaluate scientific attitude such as open mindedness, judgement ability, willingness to try experimentation, etc.

Remedial works

There will be some slow learners in a mixed ability class. So, remedial work for those who do not attain learning up to expected level has to be made. The points of difficulty can be identified through evaluation. *(The details of remedial teaching is discussed in Unit 6.)*

Summing Up

We have discussed the details of daily lesson planning; the focus was particularly on the necessary structure of lesson plan. The main points are as follows:

a) The major components of lesson plan are statement of the topic, objectives, content outline, instructional method and evaluation procedure.
b) The essential steps in lesson planning are division of lessons identification of objectives, determination of previous knowledge of content outline, selection of instructional methods, learning activities, resource materials and evaluation procedure.

UNIT 3

Pedagogical Analysis of Secondary Level Science

Chapter 6
Principles of Pedagogical Analysis

In daily teaching, the lesson plan has high importance seen earlier. While planning a lesson, we have to analyse the specific content area of that lesson. As there are different techniques for analysing the content, each of such techniques should be based on appropriate principles for analysing the pedagogy. Proper understanding of this chapter will help to analyse the content more easily and systematically.

Pedagogical analysis may be a new term for you. So first of all, we shall discuss the meaning of pedagogical analysis. Then we shall see the important principles which are the essential elements of pedagogical analysis.

Meaning

Analysis of pedagogy is not a new technique. But the new term pedagogical analysis is a new technology for a very old approach. Here pedagogical means, *a content area, which is to be instructed in any class*. For example, the content area for eighth standard science can be termed as eighth standard science pedagogy. So any given content area for any grade level can be pedagogy for the particular grade level.

While preparing the lesson plan, we should analyse the given content, for the sake of dividing them as lessons. We have already discussed the details of lesson planning in the last chapter. This chapter specially deals with one activity of lesson planning i.e, analysis of the content.

You may identify the new terms, facts, concepts and principles in a lesson while you analyse the content. But, now with the identification of the term pedagogical analysis the depth and breadth of analysis of the content has increased to a greater extent. This analysis will help the teacher to understand the essential elements of the lesson and how these elements give rise to concepts. She should also get an insight about the application of the hidden concept in new situations. Such a thorough analysis, exposing all the essential elements in the lesson such as experiments, related theories, related principles and related opinions is necessary for mastery learning. The teacher, who analyses the pedagogy in such a depth, will be able to know the pros and cons of the content.

So in essence, *pedagogical analysis can be said as the essential input for the teachers, which may include the lists of all experiments, all related principles, all related opinions and all related theories necessary for mastery learning*. A teacher could promote mastery, only if she has all the necessary information about all the essential elements of the content to be instructed. So, a thorough analysis of each of those elements is necessary. If any element is missing, mastery does not occur. As teachers, you should internalise all principles of pedagogical analysis. These principles are described in detail as follows:

Principles of Pedagogical Analysis

The important principles of pedagogical analysis are metacognition, identification of teaching strategies, content analysis, identification of attributes, exemplar planning, identification of problematic situations, mediator planning, anticipation of errors and preventive measures. All the principles are equally important while analysing the pedagogy.

Metacognition

This is the first principle of pedagogical analysis. Metacognition means the knowledge about one's thinking process. When it comes to a teacher it means how to intervene in the thinking process of learners for a better cognition, where cognition is the process of acquiring knowledge. As seen already that, our cognitive structures assimilate familiar experiences and should strive to accommodate new experience. One cannot accommodate the new knowledge, till it is linked with the existing knowledge. Here, as a teacher, one must know ones students' existing level of knowledge. Then only the teacher could help the students to comprehend new information. For example, we could not teach about computer programme to a student, who does not know what a computer is?

In order to develop the cognition of students, teacher should attach the new information on their existing knowledge. So, teacher should know how to link the new information with the existing one i.e., s/he should know how to cognise students.The teacher might have of the opinion that questioning and narration of incidents are the techniques usually adopted in classrooms for this purpose. Of course, probing questions and narration of incidents are two commonly used techniques in this regard. Along with these s/he should do other techniques such as making a list of students' existing experience, providing cues, showing a diagram or a model or actual object, group discussion, providing real life situation or verbal explanation of the situation.

Whatever technique may be arranged, the teacher should first understand the developmental stage of students and their previous knowledge. Hence, metacognition acts as a platform, only on which we could do the further analysis of the pedagogy.

Identification of Teaching Strategies

In the second principle teacher should identify the teaching strategy. Suitable teaching strategy can be selected by analysing the content of lesson and learners.

The lessons can be of various types. In a single chapter itself, there can be different types of lessons. The major types of lessons are lecture lessons, experimental lessons, discussion lessons, demonstration lessons, laboratory lessons and field study lessons. Now the question arises, how we identify the type of the lesson. We should simply analyse the pedagogy to identify the information contained in the content, which in turn helps us to identify the type of the lesson.

Suppose, for example, you are going to teach the chapter, Heredity and Variation. The introduction lesson in the chapter can be taught through a lecture type lesson. The lesson on laws of heredity can be taught through discussion, lesson on mono hybrid ratio and dihybrid ratio can be taught through experimental method, field study and observation would also help you to conclude the chapter.

Along with the types of lesson, learners are also the determining factor in the selection of teaching strategy. So, while selecting the strategy, you should take care of learners' mental level, their awareness in the process of science and their attitude towards scientific inquiry. If you do not consider the above aspects while selecting the teaching strategy, mastery learning will not occur.For example, you (teacher) cannot teach the chapter heredity and variation to those who do not know the basis of genetics. If your students are unaware of the process of science you could not select experiment and field study. So in essence, both type of lesson and learners are the determinants of teaching strategies.

Content Analysis

The main purpose of the content analysis is to identify the major concepts in the lesson. So, while analysing the content, you should concentrate to bring out major concepts. What is a concept? A concept is the major idea in the given content area. In other words, a content area is developed on the basis of an idea, namely concept.

Suppose, you are going to teach a lesson on heredity and variation, you should go through the content of the lesson and identify the concepts in the lesson are heredity, variation and genetics, which can be further, stated as follows:

Concept 1: Heredity is transmission of characteristics from parents to their offspring.

Concept 2. Variation is those differences exhibited by the offspring from their parents.

Concept 3. Genetics is the study of heredity and variation.

We have seen that the necessity of content analysis as to identify the major concepts in the content. Identification of concepts is important in the sense that our students are required to internalise the concepts through learning. Now we shall move on to the next principle of pedagogical analysis.

Identification of Attributes

This is the fourth principle of pedagogical analysis. Now you should analyse the concepts further to identify the sub concepts or attributes. Sub concepts or attributes mean the essential elements or essential parts of a concept. For example consider the concept 'two wheeler'. In order to differentiate a bicycle from a tricycle you should know the essential elements or parts of the concept two wheelers, and should also be able to understand the essential elements of three wheelers. The essential elements of two wheelers are the two wheels, handle, arrangement of seat and the mode of connection between the front and back wheels.

See another example. The colour, shape, size, texture, smell and taste are the essential elements or attributes of fruits. Difference in these attributes helps us distinguish between different types of fruits.

You should analyse the identified concept, in order to find out both the essential and non-essential attributes. Now, let us see what are essential and non-essential attributes? Let us see an example to make clear the difference between the two. The essential attributes of two wheelers are the two wheels, the body form, and the mode of connection between the front and back wheels. The handle size, colour of the body, size of the seat, sound of the horn, etc., are non-essential attributes. These are called so because these elements or attributes are not necessary to identify the concept of two wheelers.

So the essential attributes are the essential elements or characteristics that help us identify a concept and the non-essential elements are those which are not necessary to identify the concept.

Exemplar Planning

By exemplar, we mean examples. So, pre-plan all the examples which are necessary for the acquisition of new information. The planning of examples should be in terms of familiarity. Positive examples and negative examples also should be planned.

While selecting examples care should be taken to see that those are familiar to your students. For example, if you are going to teach the concept 'heredity' you may give the following as familiar examples of hereditary characters:

The eye colour and baldness in humans are the two familiar examples. You can also use skin colour of cow and calf and feather colour of hen and chicks as familiar examples.

You should be selective for positive examples and negative examples also. Here, positive example is the real example with all essential attributes and negative example means a non-example which is not an example of the given concept.

See the example of heredity. Here you can select eye colour, baldness, hair style and skin colour as positive examples. In addition to these, you should select some negative or non-examples also, which help the students to internalise the concept. You may include feeding habits, study habits, T.V. watching habits, etc. as non-examples.

Identification of Problematic Situations

In the learning of science, problems and problematic situations have a vital role to play. Usually we direct our students to such situations for concept learning. Here, problematic situation means all such situations in which the concept can be further applied. So, you should analyse the content for all such problematic situations in which the concept can be applied.For example, while you are planning to teach heredity, you should anticipate the problematic situations such as hereditary diseases, pollination, cross pollination, sexual reproduction, hybridisation and genetic engineering. So, you have to realise the situations in which the concept heredity can be applied or linked.

So, you should analyse the content in such a way to bring out any and all link or application of the concept which will result in complete and meaningful learning.

Mediator Planning

Now we move on to the seventh principle of pedagogical analysis. And this tells about pre-planning of mediators. Here, mediator stands for the situations used for developing the concept. These situations include concrete examples, anecdotes, narrations, and life situations, provided by the teacher while teaching the concept. In other words, mediators are those which act as a bridge between teacher and learner while the learning process is going on.

Suppose, you are going to teach heredity and variation. You may use the mediators such as:

1. Concrete Examples variations in characteristics of parents and children;
   - similarities among parents and their children;
   - the similarities and differences among children of the same family;

- close resemblance between identical twins;
- Life-like situations such as short films, real photographs, observation of relevant situations.
- Anecdotes on family history, resemblance among relatives and stories from epics.

All these types can be used as mediators to develop the concept of heredity and variation.

So the mediators help us to develop the concept completely which results in mastery of the given content.

Anticipation of Errors and Preventive Measures

This is the eighth and last principle of pedagogical analysis. There may be certain errors while learning any content. You have to anticipate the probable errors in learning, and to find out the preventive steps to correct those mistakes. In other words, you should find out all the possible errors in advance that can happen while learning the content. In order to locate those errors, the content should be thoroughly analysed. After anticipating the errors you should develop the preventive measures to correct those errors. So a problem will arise that, how to anticipate the possible errors? In order to anticipate the errors you should analyse the content thoroughly and locate the points at which errors can occur. Otherwise it leads to wrong learning as in the following example:

A teacher tries to explain the lethal effects of alcohol on human beings through an experiment. She takes two test tubes and puts a worm in each of the test tubes and pours about five ml of alcohol in one test tube and water in the other one. Soon the worm in the test tube containing alcohol dies. Unfortunately, the learners may get the idea that alcohol is good for destroying worms. Usually errors can occur in this way. As a result our students learn just opposite to what we intend to instruct. For example, you are going to teach heredity and variation. Let us examine the possible errors that can happen while learning the content.

- Pupils may think that heredity is different among men and women. They may also think that some have girl child because of the hereditary characters of mother.
  You can give the details of chromosomes as preventive measure to rectify misconception here.
- The difference between heredity and variation may not be clearly distinct. You should make it clear by using examples from life situations with the help of photographs of twins, siblings, close relatives, etc.

Summing Up

We have seen the meaning of pedagogical analysis and the important principles of pedagogical analysis are discussed.

The major principles are as follows:

1. Metacognition
2. Identification of teaching strategies
3. Content analysis
4. Identification of attributes
5. Exemplar planning
6. Identification of problematic situations
7. Mediator planning, and
8. Anticipation of possible errors and preventive measures.

Chapter 7
Illustrations of Pedagogical Analysis

Two illustrations explaining how to analysze the content area using the principles of pedagogical analysis are discussed. Topics from secondary level biology is taken for the purpose of analysis.

We shall discuss certain selected areas of biology content to get an insight into pedagogical analysis and its principles. The topics taken are *chemical co-ordination in plants* and *environmental pollution.*

Chemical Co-ordination in Plants

We shall analyse the pedagogy of '*Chemical co-ordination in plants*' in the light of the major principles for analysis. We will proceed through the following steps.

Step 1*: Meta cognition:* Students should know growth and flowering of plants. They might have noticed that plants near a pond grow in a curved manner towards the vacant space. So, first of all test their existing knowledge, then with the aid of photos or videos or visits or animations supplemented with verbal explanation, the concept of chemical co-ordination can be linked to pupil's existing knowledge.

Step 2*: Teaching strategy:* The lesson we have chosen is a discussion type lesson. So discussion-oriented teaching strategy can be used for instruction.

Step 3: *Content analysis:* At this step you (teacher) should read the content thoroughly. Reading should be directed to bring out the concepts hidden in the content. The concepts at this content area are as follows.

1. Plant growth is influenced by hormones
2. Hormones influence movements of plants

Step 4*: Analyses of attributes:* Analyse the concepts into sub concept level / attribute level to identify the essential and non-essential attributes or elements of the concept. In the first concept '*Plant growth is influenced by hormones*', the identified essential attributes are as follows.

a) Regarding plant growth: The progressive changes in the plant since its germination through flowering and seed formation. Hence increase in size of the plant, number and size of leaves, strength of the stem are essential attributes. The number of male and female flowers, leaves shed per day, and the number of seeds produced, etc. are non-essential attributes.

b) Hormones: The changes that occur in plants due to the scarcity or abundance of hormones. Here the essential attributes are number of flowers, length of growing regions of plants (stem and root) and the size of fruits. The non-essential attributes are the colour and size of flowers and number of petals in flowers. Now we pass on to the next step of pedagogical analysis.

Step *5: Pre-planning of examples:* Now you should select the appropriate examples including familiar examples, positive examples and negative examples. The familiar examples for plant growth are germination of seeds and its further growth, the growth of new buds, when the main stem is damaged. A positive example can be in the form of germinating seeds in a laboratory setting. Negative example for plant growth is fertilisation and pruning of plants. So you should thoroughly plan the examples to make the concept clear.

In the case of hormones, familiar and positive examples are those which are necessary for flowering of plants, and to emerge roots on plants. Negative examples are pesticides.

Step *6: Anticipation of problematic situations:* At this stage, you should identify all the situations in which the concept can be further applied. Our present context of plant growth has application in various settings such as cultivation of agricultural plants, flowering plants, and the plants cultivated for other purposes. The term hormones have application to the field of agriculture, human development and medical science. Now we shall pass on to the next step in pedagogical analysis.

Step ***7:*** *Pre Planning of mediators:* At this step teacher should plan the various mediators through which learning of the concept can be made. The suitable mediators for teaching the concept about plant growth, and experiments on seed germination and its further growth, root formation in onion bulbs, anecdotes on huge giant trees, and providing real life setting to know that different kinds of plants will grow to different size and at different rate. Hormonal influence on plant growth also can be developed through experiment as the chief mediator. Experiment can be conducted with the removal or extra provision of certain hormones to plants. Influence of hormones on animal also can be utilised in this regard.

Step *8: Anticipating possible errors and developing preventive measures:* The possible errors while learning plant growth are the following.

1. All kinds of plants grow at the same rate regardless of seasonal and geographical considerations can be a major error. You should give different examples to make the difference between the difference in growth of plants with regard to its species, season and geographical peculiarities.

2. Hormones can be used at any time of plant growth. The function of each plant hormone and the amount of which to be used at the time should also be made clear to your students. You should also give them directions that naturally addition of hormones is not necessary.

Environmental Pollution

We have already discussed one illustration of pedagogical analysis. Now, let us try to analyse the topic environmental pollution. We shall proceed through the similar steps as in the previous example.

***Step 1**: Metacognition:* Testing the existing experience of pupils is the first activity to be done in this regard. The pupils might have previous knowledge about various pollutants, and human involvement in the biosphere. You could use probing questions, verbal explanations, diagrams of biosphere destruction, newspaper articles on pollution, video clips, etc. Make them develop their existing knowledge.

***Step 2**: Teaching strategy:* Environmental pollution is a topic suitable for a field study type lesson. So the teaching should involve survey, observation, investigation and analysis of various pollutants and human involvement which leads to pollution.

***Step 3**: Content analysis:* A thorough reading of the given content of the topic will help us to identify the hidden concept. We should identify the following concepts.

1. Environmental pollution causes destruction of biosphere
2. Various pollutants and human invasion leads to pollution.

***Step 4**: Analysis of attributes:* At this step you should analyse the identified concepts into sub concepts or attributes. The first concept identified is environmental pollution causes destruction of biosphere. Now, let us examine the essential and non-essential attributes of concepts.

- Essential attributes are pollutants such as lethal gases, pesticides, detergents, chemicals, plastics and ionising radiations, production and dispersal of pollutants (for example lethal gases are bye products of our industries, which disperse through air) and the lethal effects of pollution such as different diseases, destruction of animal and plant communities, destruction of buildings and scarcity of pure water and air.
- Non-essential attributes are the scientific names of pollutants, the total amount of area polluted, the number of animals and plants affected, etc.

The second concept identified is human invasion leads to pollution. Let's examine the attributes.

The essential attributes are as follows:

1. Nature and type of human invasion – such as destruction of natural resources, production of lethal chemicals, construction of dams, improper dealing with industrial and biological wastes, etc.
2. Area of invasion – Here area referred to the total area affected and the type of area whether it has direct effect on air, land or water.
3. Amount of invasion – The amount of human involvement is another attribute. Say for example one man smokes 10 cigarettes a day means almost 40% of world population are smokers. So altogether the smoke released to the air every day is in huge amounts.

The non-essential attributes are the number of employees working in the industrial sector, their wage conditions, the number of shops selling cigarettes, etc.

***Step 5**: Pre planning of examples:* Now we pass on to the fifth step in which teacher should select appropriate examples involving familiar examples, positive examples and negative examples.

The familiar examples for environmental pollution should be selected from our own locality.

Positive examples are land pollution by pollutants such as plastics, metals, industrial wastes, and biological waste; air pollution such as Bhopal tragedy and Acid rain at many places of Europe and holes in ozone layer etc., can be used as positive examples. More local the examples the better would be the impact on learning.

Deforestation, hunting and destruction of different animals, conversion of paddy fields, and backwaters to land are non-examples or negative examples.

***Step 6**: Anticipation of problematic situation:* At this stage you should identify the situations in which the concepts can be further applied. The context of pollution has application to the field of agriculture, industry, health and sanitation, community life and education. It also has further application to the fields of conservation of nature and natural resources, and deforestation. Now we move on to the next step of pedagogical analysis.

***Step** 7: Pre planning of mediators:* At this step you should determine the mediators through which learning of concepts can be made.

Survey on various pollutants, survey on the nature of pollution at your locality, project work on environmental pollution, field trips to polluted areas, and anecdotes on harmful effects of pollution at the different parts of the world can be used as effective mediators.

Experimental studies on the effect of pollution on biosphere also are an effective mediator. Now we move on to the final step of pedagogical analysis.

Step 8: *Anticipating possible errors and developing preventive measures*

You might have thought of possible errors that may occur during the learning of the content at this stage. Let us see what are those errors and how do we prevent such errors.

1. One may think that if I put a plastic bag in soil, it will not destroy the texture of soil, as bag is very small when compared to the soil mass.
   You must remind pupils through examples, that such 'ones' together to aggregate as hundreds of kilogrammes of waste materials to the soil.
2. Another error may be at the point that fertilisers and pesticides are essential for agriculture. Of course they are essential but the amount to be used, how to use and when to use are highly significant as far as pollution is concerned. You could prevent this error by highlighting biological control of pests, and natural farming of crops, etc., through discussion.
   These may be the possible errors that may happen while learning the content.

UNIT 4

Instructional Strategies in Science

CHAPTER 8
Concept Attainment Model

In teaching of science, models of teaching have significant role to play. Concept Attainment model, Advance Organiser model, Biological Science Inquiry model, Cognitive Growth model, Group Investigation model, and Mastery Learning models are discussed here. Each model has basic common structural details such as *syntax, social system, principles of reaction, and support system.*

- Syntax of the model comprises of the phases of model and each model has different phases.
- Social system describes the role of students and teachers.
- Principles of reaction explain the procedure by which teacher deals with the reactions of students.
- Support system deals with the use of other teaching aids, human skills and technical facilities required for the instruction using the model.

Concept Attainment Model

'Concept' is a familiar term for us, but the term concept attainment may be new one. This model of teaching is proposed by J. Brunner, for developing concept by prescribing its examples and non-examples. This chapter also includes the essential elements of the model, application and effects of the model.

This model belongs to the information processing family of teaching models. This family includes models that help students to process information received from their environment. This model includes methods and theories which are specifically helpful in processing information. Now let us see the meaning of concept attainment.

Meaning

The major function of schooling is helping children to learn concepts efficiently. Concept is an idea, constituted by interlinking facts. The learning of anything involves thinking, so also the learning of concepts. Brunner, et al describes thinking as categorising. Let us see an example to understand categorising.

A teacher is trying to teach about mammals. She presents the major characteristics of mammals. Then she gives list of animals and asks the students to choose mammals from the list. They are able to point out the mammals by grouping the animals into different groups based on their common characteristics.

This categorisation involves two processes, namely, identifying and classifying based on certain criteria. Such categorisation leads to concept formation. In the above example, the concept is that of mammals. Thus, in general, categorising means understanding a concept, hence, the first step of concept attainment. Concept attainment is a higher state of knowledge, which means understanding concepts by all its essential details and able to describe it in our own words.

Model of Teaching

The concept attainment model of teaching considers mainly two aspects.

- Nature of concepts, and
- Thinking processes to learn concepts

Nature of concepts: Structure of knowledge is comprised of concepts and Burner suggests five elements for any concept as under.

i. *Name*: It is a term standing for the concept, i.e., name of the concept — Fruit, bird, car, etc. are names.

ii. *Examples:* This refers to the positive and negative examples of the concept. For concept attainment, recognition of positive examples and distinguishing them from negative examples is necessary. Suppose, we put an array of mangoes of same variety, and one or two apples and oranges are also placed among them. Here, then, apple and oranges are negative examples for the concept of 'Mangoes'.

iii. *Attributes:* Attributes mean common characteristic features of an object. These attributes help us to identify such objects and classify it into a particular concept. For example, we know orange, mango, apple and grapes are fruits among the group of potato, cabbage, beans and radish. Here we identify certain common or distinguishing or essential characteristics of fruits, which help us to attain the concept of fruits such as fleshy, sweet, change in colour while ripen etc. So, concept attainment involves distinguishing essential attributes from non-essential ones.

iv. *Attribute Values:* Each essential attributes have a range of value in itself, which help us to distinguish it. The colour of apple has a range of values from green to yellow, golden to red, etc. to define it as ripe and eatable. If these range of colours has not appeared, we consider them as inedible. So, colour, shape, size or any other attribute of objects may vary between a range. And this range is referred to as the attribute values.

v. *The Rule:* A rule is a definition or statement of a concept. For example, fruits are fleshy, juicy and edible is a rule for the concept fruit. The rule forms towards the end of the concept attainment process and it indicates all the essential attributes of a concept. Now we shall have a look at the duties of a teacher while presenting a concept.

Role of the Teacher: As seen attributes play an important role in distinguishing one concept from another. The difference in combination of attributes helps us to distinguish between orange and apple. Here, teacher's role is to identify all the five elements of the concept. Among these elements we should first identify the essential attributes and differentiate it from the non-essential attributes. Then carefully choose the positive examples, which should include all the essential attributes. Some negative examples also should be selected. You should take care to eliminate all the unnecessary or noisy information from the examples. These examples should be designed in such a way that all the essential attributes will be clearly present in them. You should select some additional examples also to facilitate the concept attainment process. Three steps can be adopted to check whether pupils attain a concept. Ask students to describe the concept in terms of all the essential attributes as first step; as second step, ask them to distinguish between examples and non-examples, and to generate their own examples as third step. If students successfully do these steps, we should decide that they have attained the concept.

It is the role of the teacher to determine the appropriate thinking strategy for concept attainment.

Thinking Strategies for Concept Attainment

Here, strategy means the decision making activity to attain a concept. We should follow certain thinking processes, which lead to decision making. Such thinking strategies are always different for different types of concepts. In simple terms, thinking strategy means the various activities that are undertaken by an individual to learn a concept meaningfully. Say for example, the concept of weight difference of different objects can be attained using different activities such as (i) comparing weight of one object with other objects, or (ii) find out the weight of each object and understand the difference, or (iii) comparing the weight of each item with a standard weight.

These are three thinking strategies which help a learner to attain the concept. Thinking strategy can be different from concept to concept and learner to learner. Hence, opportunity to explore different strategies should be made available for attaining a concept. In concept attainment teaching, two learning conditions are used generally, namely *reception oriented and selection oriented.*

Reception condition: In this condition, teacher provides examples of a concept by marking them 'yes' or 'no', depending on the presence or absence of the concept in the example ('yes' stands for positive example and 'no' for negative example). Here pupils' effort will be low, as they have to receive what is given by the teacher. For example, teacher decides to teach the concept tap root system. She may provide examples of tap root system and fibrous root system marking 'yes' and 'no' respectively. Differentiating between the two will be then easy for the pupils.

Selection conditions: It is, as the name indicates, selecting positive and negative examples ('yes' and 'no') from a group of examples which are not marked as 'yes' or 'no'. Here pupils have to select (identify) each example and should inquire whether it is a positive example or not. Teacher may give some plants to her pupils to attain the concept of tap root system. The plants given as examples include both types, with tap root system and fibrous root system. So, pupils have to inquire on each example by matching it with the essential attributes of tap root system, in order to identify it as positive or negative example.

The reception strategy will help us to teach the elements of concepts well. But if you want your pupils to apply their own initiation and control, selection strategy is useful. And of course a third condition for real life, such as 'unorganised data' will help the pupils to transfer the concept in to real life situations. Now, we pass on to the application and effects of concept attainment model of teaching.

Application of Concept Attainment Model

Now, let us trace out the various applications of this model.

i) The model is applicable to all age levels and grade levels. The reception model is more advantageous for elementary learning and the selection and unorganised material model are better for secondary and higher levels.
ii) This model helps inductive learning.
iii) This model is also used as an effective tool for evaluation. It helps us to determine whether students have mastered the ideas that are already taught to them.
iv) This is also helpful in developing an attitude of inquiry in students.

Effects of Concept Attainment Model of Teaching

We have adopted this model to obtain certain specific instructional effects. This model is designed for instruction on the nature of concepts and on specific concepts. So this will help the students to analyse the concept in all its details. Along with it, the model encourages students to improve their thinking strategies and to develop awareness in alternative perspectives for learning concepts. These are the effects of concept attainment model of teaching.

Types of Concept Attainment Model

There are three types of concept attainment teaching models namely reception oriented, selection oriented and unorganised material model. Each model involves syntax, social system, principles of reaction and support system.

1. Reception-oriented Model of Concept Attainment

Concept attainment model has three phases. The first part of the model is termed as syntax.

Syntax

It involves three phases of activity.

Phase I: Presentation of data and identification of concepts: You should arrange the examples (having attributes of the concept) and non-examples (in which the attributes of the concept will not be present) in such a way, that the pupils should be able to identify the attributes and thereby the concept. Let us see an example. Teacher is trying to develop the concept — petals of a flower. Teacher instructs the students that, certain passages are given on the basis of a concept in her mind about parts of flower. Some examples are marked 'yes' and others marked 'no' on the basis of whether the concept is present or not in the example.

Example 1

'Yes' A part of flower, which is the most attractive part of garden plants.

Example 2

'No' Leaves, fruits, tubers, and stem of plants have various uses and have economic importance according to the demand.

Example 3

'Yes' They appear in beautiful colours. But those at night are usually white in colour. The actual function is to attract pollinating agents.

Example 4

'No' The sepals are unattractive in colour and shape, but have an important role to play by supporting other parts of the flower.

From these examples, your pupils should be able to identify the concept in the mind of teacher, as the "petals of flowers".

Phase II: Testing Attainment of concepts: In this phase, you should present unlabeled examples and ask the students to identify the correct examples from the group of positive and negative ones. When they succeeded in identifying the positive examples then they are directed to suggest examples of their own. This will help the learner to get information about the concept.

Phase III: Analysis of thinking strategies: At this stage, your students try to analyse the thinking strategies used to attain the concept. They themselves should test and verify which strategy is appropriate and at what time. Here, strategy stands for the methodology by which one could attain the concept easily.

Social System

Social system describes activities of teacher while teaching with reception model. You should select the concept first, then organise the material into positive and negative examples and put them in sequential order. While designing the examples, you should take utmost care to make clear the attributes of the concept. You should also record students' responses and provide additional information, if required.

Principles of Reaction

This part of the model describes how you should react to the responses of the students. You should give a supportive environment for students, while you are teaching with reception model. You should help the students to test their thinking strategies and encourage them to attempt various strategies for the attainment of the concept.

Support System

This part of the model describes the additional supports and aids, necessary for teaching using the model. Concepts are embedded in concept attainment lessons. So the students' role is to attain the hidden concepts, with the aid of positive and negative examples. The students are also directed to note down the attributes in the examples given to them. Hence, well chosen examples will be the essential support system for this model.

2. Selection- Oriented Model of Teaching

The selection-oriented model is similar to that of reception model in many aspects, but there are differences in some aspects of phase I of the model. The differences are as follows.

1. In selection model the examples are unlabeled.
2. The students should inquire into the examples to know whether it is 'yes' or 'no'.

3. It is the duty of the students to sequence the examples.
4. Responsibility for concept attainment and attribute tracking is in the hands of the students.

Suppose, the teacher is going to develop the concept of fleshy fruits. So, a variety of fleshy fruits such as mango, apple, papaya, etc. are provided along with cashew nut and beans as unlabeled examples. Then the teacher asks students to identify the concept in her/his mind from the given objects. By comparing the important characteristics (here essential attributes) of the given examples, the students shall identify that many of the examples belong to one group (i.e. here fleshy fruits). So, in order to understand the correctness of their conclusion, students take each example and categorise it as a positive example or negative example. The teacher will say 'yes' or 'no' according to the correctness of students' claims. By the end of this process, students will be able to identify the concept and essential attributes, so as to facilitate concept formation. Finally, the teacher can introduce name of the concept.

Phase II and III are similar to the Reception-Oriented model.

3. *Unorganised Materials Model*

Here the students are exposed to real life situations or to unorganised (disarrange, unlabeled) data.

Syntax

The model has only two phases.

Phase I: Description of concept is as it is used: In this phase the students are required to locate and label concept. They should also identify the attributes of the given concept.

Phase II: Evaluation of concept. In this phase, the students have a discussion on the adequacy and appropriateness of the concepts used. They should also compare the examples with other data to check the appropriateness to the concept.

The *social system, principles of reaction* and *support system* are similar to that of the reception model.

Unorganised material model is usually used for the instruction of adult learners. The learning tasks should be in the form of assignment questions or self work exercises. Individual students can work on such questions by collecting data from all available sources. Because these data are spread out in all these sources, that is, they are unorganised. Hence, it is called as unorganised material model. Each student should analyse the data obtained from various sources and conclude their findings as a concept.

A sample assignment title for this model is as follows:

"The use of biological control as a means of pest control."

Summing Up

We discussed the important aspects of 'concept attainment' model of teaching. Concept attainment means identifying concept by all its details and be able to describe it in one's own words. We have also seen the nature of concepts in terms of its name, examples, attributes, attribute values and rule. Teacher has to play an important role in concept attainment. Two thinking strategies, such as reception conditions, and selection conditions, were also discussed. Reception model of concept attainment has three phases: phase I, presentation of data and identification of concepts; phase II, testing attainment of concept; and phase III, analysis of thinking strategies. We have also discussed selection and unorganised material model of concept attainment. This model helps the instruction of concepts, develops thinking strategies of students and let them know about alternate ways of learning a concept.

CHAPTER 9

Advance Organiser Mode

Advance organiser' may be really a new term. This model is proposed by David P. Ausubel. Ausubel put forth this model to help convey large amount of information as meaningful and efficient as possible. This model aims at strengthening students' learning ability. It is essential for teachers to understand various aspects of advance organisers to improve the lecture type presentations. Advance organiser model also belongs to the information processing family of teaching model.

Meaning

Advance organisers are introductory materials present ahead of the learning task which aim to relate the new concept with the already developed concepts. It acts as a bridge between the already learned material and the new material to be learned. The advance organiser may be concepts, terms, and appropriate illustrations. For example, you want your students to acquire information about food chain. You will not present the matter directly to the students. Instead of that you will say about different types of animals and their feeding habits and the categories of herbivorous, carnivorous and omnivorous animals. All these things we refer to as previous knowledge that is necessary to learn the new material. Brushing up of the previous knowledge helps your students to internalise the new and additional information. So, in simple terms advance organiser is the bit of information, which is already familiar for learners and presented ahead of new information.

Types of Advance Organisers

Ausubel proposed two types of advance organisers on the basis of familiarity of students with the learning material. They are—expository, and comparative advance organisers.

Expository Advance Organiser: Expository organisers are used with unfamiliar materials. Here a general outline is given as advance organiser. For example, if we want to instruct about groups of trees, first of all begin with kinds of forests, then sub-forest, different types of trees and plants and the land area in which specific trees are seen. Then only you should introduce group of trees. Here the expository advance organiser helps to introduce unfamiliar information in a deductive manner.

Comparative Advance Organiser: This is mostly used with relatively familiar learning material. Comparative advance organiser aim at integrating new concepts with the already existing concepts. They are also designed in such a way to discriminate between old concepts, i.e., by exploring its similarity and differences. Suppose you are going to teach respiration in human beings, you could use comparative advance organiser in this regard. Respiration in fishes is familiar to students, which could be used to explore the details of respiration in human beings, by comparing with that of fishes.

Ausubel proposed advance organiser to increase the effectiveness of lectures and thereby promote meaningful learning. And according to him, an introductory portion in the form of advance organiser is essential for meaningful verbal learning.

Advance Organiser Model of Teaching

The structural details of the model is the same as that of the concept attainment model such as syntax, social system, principles of reaction, and support system.

Syntax

The advance organiser model has three phases.

Phase I: Presentation of advance organizer: At this phase you (teacher) should present the advance organiser. First of all aims and objectives of the lesson should be explained. This is helpful to get students' attention and help to facilitate meaningful learning.

Then you should present the advance organiser. While presenting the organiser, take care of the following aspects:

1. You should not confuse the organiser with your daily lesson introduction.
2. Determine whether it is expository or comparative in which the essential features of the concept would be pointed out. The presentation of the organiser should be short.
3. The essential attributes should be highlighted.
4. Examples should be used to explain the attributes.
5. You should repeat many times the new or special terminology.
6. The awareness of prior knowledge of learners would be prompted to develop the necessary cognitive structure in them. These are the activities to be performed by the teacher in phase I.

Phase II: Presentation of learning task: The actual learning material is presented at this phase in the form of lectures, discussion, films, experiments or reading. You should take care of two tasks at this phase. They are:

1. to maintain students' attention, and
2. logical organisation of the learning material

Various techniques such as discussion, films, and experiments will be helpful to maintain students' attention.

Now we move on to the phase III of the model.

Phase III: Strengthening cognitive organization: At this phase, you shall test the relationship of learning material to the existing ideas. You should plan for activities in this respect. Those activities are as follows.

a) Promoting integrative reconciliation
b) Promoting active reception learning
c) Principle approach to knowledge
d) Clarification.

a) *Integrative reconciliation* means integration of new information with the existing cognitive structure. You should adopt several ways to facilitate reconciliation. They are:

1. to remind students about the ideas presented;
2. to ask students to give the summary of major attributes of new learning material;
3. to repeat definitions precisely; and
4. ask the students to bring out the differences between different aspects of the material.

b) *Active reception learning***:** You should promote active learning also using some of the following activities:

i) Asking students to describe, how the new learning material is related to the existing knowledge.
ii) Asking students to give additional examples.
iii) Asking students to give the essence of the new learning material in their own words.
iv) Asking students to examine the learning material from alternative points of view.

All these activities are to be done by the students after receiving the learning material from the teacher; hence it is reception learning, though it is actively done.

c) *Principle approach to knowledge* can also be promoted in this model. In this respect, you should guide the students to recognise assumptions or inferences of the learning material. And also to judge and challenge these inferences.

d) *Clarification* of various aspects should be done by the teacher. Students should have doubts about additional or new information or application of any idea. At this stage you have to give response to clarify the doubts of students. The teacher also has other roles to perform while teaching with advance organiser.

Role of the Teacher

As a teacher, you have to play some very important roles. The most important role is to develop the advance organiser. While developing an advance organiser you should integrate the concept in the new learning material. Firstly, you should be thorough with the new learning material and its organisation. You must decide the sequencing of information in the given subject area. The similarities, differences, essential attributes and examples selected should be suitable. While developing the learning material, you should consider the experiences and intellectual background of your students. And at the final stage you must give enough support to your students, so that they can internalise the new information meaningfully.

These are some of the important points that you should bear in mind while teaching using advance organiser model. And now, we shall move on to the social system of the model.

Social System

In social system, you have control of the structure of learning and have to relate continuously to the new learning material. You should give enough help to the students so that they can differentiate new information from existing information. In the third phase of the model, it turns out to more interactive sessions as students may raise many questions and comments. The success of this model depends on the learners' desire to integrate the new information with the existing knowledge and on the nature of your presentation and organisation of material.

Principle of Reaction

The teacher's responses to the learners' reaction will be directed for clarifying the meaning of new learning material. Differentiation between the aspects should be made clear. The reconciliation of new information with the existing information also is very important. This will help your students to develop a critical approach to knowledge. Here also, students have the initiative role in learning the new material. Now, we shall move on to the support system of the model.

Support System

As a well organised material is the backbone of this model, so the material itself is the support requirement. The advance organiser used for the meaningful learning of the information is developed in such a way, that it will integrate with the existing knowledge. The success of which depends on the relationship between the organiser and the content.

Application of the Model

The instructional applications of the model are given as follows

- The advance organiser model is useful to instruct systematically the key ideas of a topic in a step wise manner.
- This is helpful to increase learner's factual information.
- You should teach the skill of effective reception learning. The students should apply these techniques on their own.
- Advance organiser is useful for the presentation, renewal and clarification of ideas or information.

Effects of the Model

You are familiar with the instructional effects of the model. They are the strength of conceptual structures and meaningful assimilation of concepts. Ausubel also points out that it helps to foster inquiry and precise thinking habits.

Summing Up

We discussed the important aspects of advance organiser model of teaching. There are two types of advance organisers, namely expository and comparative advance organisers. Advance organiser is the material given at the beginning of a learning task, in order to link the new idea with the existing ideas.

The syntax of this model has three phases.

Phase I: Presentation of advance organiser

Phase II: Presentation of learning task, and

Phase III: Strengthening cognitive organisation

The role of the teacher is very crucial in this model as s/he is responsible to develop the advance organiser. The success of this model depends on the presentation and organisation of the material. The model is helpful in the instruction of large classes. Systematic instruction should be given systematically using the model. This model helps to strengthening of conceptual structures and meaningful assimilation of concepts and ideas.

Chapter 10
Biological Science Inquiry Model

Biological science inquiry model is proposed by Joseph Schwab and is based on the Biological Science Curriculum Study.

Meaning of Inquiry

Nowadays, science is considered more as a process than a product. So the process for the ways of acquiring knowledge is important because the product or results depend on it. For example, when some of your students were playing on the ground, they incidentally noticed stones here and there on the ground. When they removed the stones, they noticed that the colour of the grass under the stones changed into yellow. Why does it happen so? What is the truth behind this? These are the questions to be answered. In order to answer these questions we should thoroughly inquire into the different aspects of the observation. So the search for what had happened can be termed as inquiry. The essential attribute of science is inquiry. Inquiry helps us to explore the details of the various aspects of a process and thereby its product.

How to Develop Inquiry Attitude

Now we shall discuss about how we can develop inquiry attitude in our students. In the previous example, we saw a problem situation and to solve the problem invite our students to inquiry. While teaching science, always we begin with a problematic or puzzling situation and then help our students to explore the process behind the situation. For example, you are going to teach human respiratory system. You shall narrate an incident. A five year old boy, whose ball fell into a pond and he jumped into the pond, though he did not know how to swim. What will happen then? Your students will say that he will die. You may raise a question — Why does he die? That is the next problem. Thus, a situation has been created, and now you should guide or direct your students to inquire into the various aspects of the situation.

In addition to this, you should invite your students to inquiry with the aid of specially designed statements, which express the tentative nature of science. The following statements can be useful in this regard. "We do not know", "We are unable to discover how this happens", "The evidence about this is contradictory", "It needs further inquiry", "There exists difference of opinion". All these statements are helpful to express the changing nature of science and thereby to promote inquiry attitude.

Organisation of laboratory works will help you to foster inquiry. Every child should inquire individually and in groups with reference to the nature of the problem. For example, if your students are directed to find out the pH value of soil samples of different areas of your locality, the students can do this work individually or in small groups. Such experiments have profound influence in promoting inquiry.

These are the various activities that can help to promote inquiry attitude in your students.

Model of Teaching

The model of teaching aims to involve your students in inquiry by inviting them to any area of investigation. You as the teacher, should help your students to identify the problem and design the ways to solve the problematic situation. This type of inquiry will help students to internalise the systematic way of knowing. As in the case of the two models discussed earlier, this model also proceeds in the same format. Inquiry may be directed towards processes such as collection of data, analysis of data and interpretation of data.

Syntax

The syntax of this model includes four phases. Each of these phases may have different sequences.

Phase I: Posing an area of investigation: At the first phase, an area of investigation is revealed to the student. You should give directions for various methodologies to be used for the given area of investigation.For example, you have selected the area of investigation, 'soil pH and agricultural crops'. Here the methodologies such as laboratory work, experimental method survey of different locality and crop production can be successfully done.

Phase II: Structuring of problem: At this phase, you should give necessary directions to your students to structure the problem and to identify the difficulty in the investigation. The difficulty on which the investigation is to be done might involve the sources of data, the collection of data, method of data collection, data interpretation and hypothesis testing.

Phase III: Identification of problem in the investigation: At this phase, the students are asked to speculate about the problem. This speculation will help them to postulate a tentative solution for the problem. The difficulties to solve the problem and to attain the final solution could be realised at this phase. For example, when your students are asked to speculate about the problem of soil pH and crop production, they will be able to feel the actual problem related between soil pH and crop production, involved in the inquiry.

Phase IV: Suggesting ways to solve the problems: At this phase your students are asked to think about the possible ways to solve the problem. They should decide the methodology to be adopted. And if necessary, they should redesign the experiment to organise new ways to generate data and collection of data. Here they do not conduct actual investigation, but only preparation for it. Using either of these ways, the students have to clear up the problematic situation.

Social System

While you are teaching with this model, the classroom climate will be co-operative in nature. Here the students are invited to inquiry. Teacher acts only as a guide or facilitator of learning. The students have the major role to play. They have to formulate hypothesis, develop inquiry designs and should redesign as and when required.

Principles of Reaction

In this model, you have the role of a director, a guide or a promoter of inquiry. You should give necessary directions to the students to channelise the inquiry through the right path. You should also help them to formulate hypothesis, locating sources of data, collection and interpretation of data.

Support System

The support system, first of all, demands a flexible and skilled instructor (here, you) to the process of inquiry. You should be flexible in the sense that you should be able to mobilise your plans differently as per your students' needs and you should also have a masterly approach to inquiry. Secondly, the model demands real life like areas of investigation and problems. In addition to these, there will be need of necessary sources of data.

Application of the Model

This model has wider applicability, but unfortunately, we are not exploiting this in our classrooms. Since it is inquiry oriented, we usually try to keep it away, as we have to save time.

This model can be applied to the nature of design of text books. We could design them as invitation to inquiry type text books. This model will help in designing the instructional material in such a way where learning can be maximised.

This model has applicability to other disciplines also. But a precondition is there that the instructors must be knowledgeable in practising this model.

Effects of the Model

This model is primarily designed to teach the process of science and thereby research in biology. Your students will have to develop a commitment to scientific inquiry through this method. They, of course, have chances to develop open-mindedness through this model. In addition to these, this model fosters a spirit of co-operation and ability to work with others.

These are the major effects of the biological science inquiry model.

Summing Up

We discussed the important aspects of biological science inquiry model. Inquiry means systematic search of truth (knowledge). Inquiry attitude can be developed by providing necessary activities including laboratory work. The model of teaching involves syntax, social system, principles of reaction and support system. The syntax have four phases: phase I is revealing the area of investigation; phase II structuring the problem; phase III identification of the actual problem difficulty; and phase IV suggesting ways to solve the problem.

Classroom climate for this model should be co-operative. Teacher should be a guide in this model. The support system demands highly flexible and creative instructor.

Biological science inquiry model has many applications. Textbooks can be developed with inbuilt invitation to inquiry. Inquiry promotes mastery learning, and can be applied to other disciplines also. This model mainly aims to teach process of science, and to develop co-operation, open-mindedness, and inquiry attitude.

CHAPTER 11
Cognitive Growth Model

Cognitive Growth model is developed by Jean Piaget. This chapter involves a teaching model which fosters the cognitive development of students based on the principles of cognitive growth. It is necessary to have an understanding of cognitive growth model to cater to the intellectual needs of students at the secondary level.

We have already discussed three models of teaching belonging to the family of information processing teaching models. This model is also based on the cognitive abilities of the learner. The description of cognitive growth model is given in the same order as that of the other models discussed so far.

Meaning of Cognitive Growth

As discussed earlier, cognitive development, according to Piaget, is the transition from one cognitive stage to next and thereby reaching the final stage of development. In the course of life, one comes across varied experiences as assimilated into their present behaviour pattern, and new information triggers change in the existing cognitive structure and thereby promotes cognitive growth.

So, the change in cognitive structure to accommodate the new information can be termed as cognitive growth. The cognitive growth is age dependent, and has direct relation to the environment in which the individual exists. For example, a three year old baby does not know the details of music, but she could respond to familiar music and differentiate new or strange music and sounds. If the child does not get any opportunity to listen to music, she cannot understand it.

In essence, cognitive growth means expansion of cognitive structure of an individual which helps his development from one cognitive developmental stage to the other. While you are teaching, you must provide appropriate environment for your students to promote their cognitive growth.

Principles of Teaching

On the basis of the Piagetian theory of development, we have to consider the following principles, while teaching through this model.

1. Development is the function of experience and maturation.
2. We have already discussed that experience is essential for development. Along with experience, physical maturation is also

essential for development. For example, you give tricycle training to a young child. The child will not ride the tricycle properly until s/he is physically mature to do that.

3. Teaching is creation of environments: This is the second principle to be considered, while teaching for cognitive growth. Our aim is to give necessary experience and practice to students in specific mental operations. When we are teaching a new term, we should recite it a number of times, so that our students are able to spell it correctly by listening to our recitation.
4. Learning is an active process: The third principle says that learning occurs only when the learner is active. We should give as much examples and objects to keep the students active. When you intend to teach about the parts of a flower, the learners become very active if you bring some flowers into the class.
5. Different types of knowledge require different learning situations: According to Piaget, knowledge is of three types namely physical, social and logical. And the learning situation for each type of knowledge is different from one another. You should teach the physical knowledge about flower such as its colour, smell, parts and season when it appears, by using the actual object, or its photograph. But is there any social knowledge for flowers? Think of the uses of flowers in social situations. So the social knowledge is its uses for decoration, marriages, etc. Now, what is the logical knowledge? Social knowledge is received by free interaction with others, but logical knowledge is obtained through experimenting and questioning.

These are the major principles to be considered while teaching for cognitive growth.

Model of Teaching

This model of teaching is based on the principles of Piagetian theory. In this model, you have to give tasks to students to determine the cognitive development stage of each child. Once you have determined the cognitive development stage of children, you could teach them using this model, with the following aspects.

Syntax

The syntax of this model consists of three phases. Let us see the phases one by one.

Phase I: Confrontation with stage relevant tasks: At this phase, you should present a puzzling situation to the students. While developing the situation, you should take care of the following aspects. The situation should be designed in accordance with the learners' developmental stage.

The content of the situation should contain familiarity and newness at the same time. This will help the students to assimilate the existing experience and to accommodate the new experience.

Phase II: Inquiry: In this phase your students are required to make responses in connection with the puzzling situation to which they are exposed in Phase I. Then the students are required to forward their justifications in connection with their responses. At this time you should direct the students by probing questions and counter suggestions.For example, the puzzling situation is that leaves of a plant kept in a dark room for two days, when tested for glucose give a negative result. The students have already learned photosynthesis. Then you ask for student's responses. Some of them would say it is due to the absence of heat, some others would say absence of wind and yet another group would say that it is due to the absence of light. In order to get these responses you should ask questions such as "What do you think?", "What do you see?", "What is your opinion?", and "Is it your opinion?", etc. Then you should ask them to justify their responses. The questions such as "Why do you think so?", "Why you say so?" etc. are seeking such justifications. You should ask probing questions as per justifications of students. Such as, if one student answered as 'light' you can ask "What about wind?", "What about heat". This will help the students to verify their responses and enable them to correct it if any misconceptions are there.

Phase III: Transfer: Third phase is the transfer phase. At this phase, you should provide additional similar situations to the students and ask them to provide reason for each. If the students' responses are appropriate, then you can make sure that the students could apply their learning to new situations. For example, in the previous example your students realised that light is essential for photosynthesis. After that it will be very easy for them to infer that carbon dioxide is essential for photosynthesis.

Social System

The structuring of social system can range from minimum to highly structured type. Teacher creates an environment, in which the students are required to perform. But your role is only as a guide in the process of student's inquiry. The intellectual and social climate of the class is free and open.

Principles of Reaction

According to Piaget, the teacher has three roles, namely,

1) Organiser of learning environment,
2) Assessor of children's thinking, and
3) Initiator of group activities.

As an organiser of learning environment, you should develop such an environment, in which your students feel free and respond naturally. You should take care to avoid a leading role in learning. Another thing, you should consider is the selection of learning situation, which should match with the learner's developmental level. While the students are reasoning, you should help them reach the correct response.

Support System

The support system for this model involves a conducive environment and a skilled teacher. You should develop environment as the developmental stage of the students. You should also get ready with a list of counter-suggestions to channelise students to the correct response. As a teacher, you should facilitate learning by offering appropriate stimulating comments at suitable time.

Application of the Model

According to Piaget, this model aims at developing selected aspects of cognitive development. Along with the instructional aim, this model also helps the development such as reasoning, making judgments, etc. and socio-emotional development.

Summing up

The details of cognitive growth model are discussed. Cognitive growth means expansion of cognitive structure, The principles of teaching on the basis of the Piagetian theory are discussed. They are:

I. development is the function of experience and maturation,
II. teaching is creation of environment,
III. learning is an active process, and
IV. different types of knowledge require different learning situations.

This model also has syntax, social system, principles of reaction and support system. The syntax has three phases. Phase I is confrontation with stage relevant task, phase II inquiry, and phase III transfer. Cognitive growth model is applicable for cognitive development and social development.

Chapter 12
Group Investigation Model

Human beings are social beings; we cannot live without the help of other members in the community. Here, we will get the details of a model of teaching, which operates in such a social set up. The proponent of this model is Herbret Thelen. As teachers, it is essential to understand the important concepts of group investigation model of teaching, the details of which follow.

Meaning

According to Thelen, humans are basically social, who cannot live without the assistance of other members of the society. Similarly, our classrooms are also considered as a society which has its own social characteristics. Since the classroom is a society, the learning process will naturally be a group activity. Thelen considers classroom as miniature democracy also. So, naturally the principles of democracy should be followed in the process of learning also. Here, the learners as a group should identify the problem and investigate on it. All the students should have to play a role in such investigation. In simple terms, group investigation means inquiry on a problem by a group as a whole. Now we shall pass on to the basic concepts of group investigation.

Basic Concepts of Group Investigation

There are some basic concepts for Thelen's group investigation strategy. They are:

1. Inquiry
2. Knowledge, and
3. Dynamics of the learning group.

We shall discuss these concepts one by one:

Inquiry

We have already seen the various aspects on inquiry in the previous chapter, Biological Science Inquiry model. The situation which demands inquiry is the same as that of the cognitive growth model, i.e. exploration of a puzzling situation. According to Thelen, inquiry is at the heart of group investigation; the students are able to develop participative behaviour.

Knowledge

The second concept of group investigation is knowledge. Knowledge brings forth changes in past experience and brings up present experience. Along with knowledge of results, knowledge of emotions and personal needs also can be generated through group investigation.

Dynamics of the learning group

Thelen remarked that a teachable group is necessary for group investigation. A teachable group means a group of ten to fifteen students of the same class confronted with a puzzling situation. The readiness of the students should be communicative to each other and should have an awareness of "What to do" and "How to do".

Suppose, you have directed your students to a puzzling situation. Here the situation is two leaves from a plant tested for the presence of glucose. One of them was covered with black paper and the other exposed to sun light. The one which was covered showed negative result. Now your students are exposed to a problematic situation. They form a group and analyse their past experiences. They have already learned photosynthesis. They discuss and develop suitable design for solving the problem. In the course of time you should give necessary directions to help them to conduct inquiry.

Model of Teaching

This model of teaching has the same structural details of the models we have already discussed. Now we shall discuss each of these aspects in the same sequential order.

Syntax

The syntax of this model is fairly longer than those we have discussed earlier. It has six phases.

Phase I: Confrontation of puzzling situation: Phase I is the same as that of the phase I of cognitive growth model. Here also students are exposed to a problematic situation at first. The presentation of the situation may take place verbally or it may be an actual experience. For example, you are going to introduce sunlight that is essential for photosynthesis by creating a situation. You shall narrate the experiment verbally or you can conduct the experience in your classroom. In the latter case, students are exposed to the actual situation.

Phase II: Exploration of reactions: At this phase, you should invite various reactions of your students regarding the puzzling situation. You should help the students to draw their attention to the difference in reactions made by them. For example, in an experiment to test light is essential for photosynthesis, responses such as 'temperature is essential', light is essential', etc., might have been forwarded by your students. You have to draw everyone's attention to each of these responses.

Phase III: Formulation and structuring of the problem: While listening to the differences in opinion, your students will be interested to explore the true knowledge from these relations. At this phase, you should direct them to formulate and structure the problem. While formulating the problem, students should be aware of what is to be inquired. (i.e. the actual problem). When structuring the problem, different aspects of inquiry, and difficulties of the inquiry may be taken into consideration.

Take the example of sunlight which is essential for photosynthesis. At the third phase, you should help the students to formulate the actual problem and plan what all steps are to be involved and what all materials are necessary to investigate into the problem.

Phase IV: Independent and group study: After formulating and structuring the problem, students analyse each one's role to organise the activities required for each role. Then they should act as per their roles, and find out their results and report it.

In the experiment for sunlight that is essential for photosynthesis, each one can investigate into a single reaction mentioned in phase II to find out the correct solution. Then, report the result of each one's observation.

Phase V: Analyse progress and process: At this stage the group analyses the findings of different individuals and the process by which they reach the final solution.

The group analyses the result of each individual's inquiry i.e. the experiments to see whether wind is essential or temperature is essential or light is essential. And they also analyse how each of them carried out the inquiry.

Phase VI: Recycle activity: At this phase the group is exposed to a new puzzling situation or to a problem arose while investigating the previous problem. The same process is repeated to find out the new knowledge.

In our example, a new problem arising may be any other factors essential for photosynthesis or a new problem can be identification of the gas evolved during photosynthesis.

Social System

The social system is democratic type. So the relation between the members of the group is very important. Activities of the group is important than that of individuals. The teacher does not interfere much in the structuring of the group investigation. The status of both students and teacher is the same, because in democracy there is no status differentiation.

Principle of Reaction

You have to perform the role of facilitator of learning in the forms of a counsellor, consultant and a friendly critic. You should help them to understand the difference in the reaction made by them, help them to the formulation and structuring of the inquiry and to guide them to conduct the investigation in the right way. In addition to these, you should guide them to internalise the experience of the group in three levels namely,

- Problem solving level (Nature of problem, and factors involved in)
- Group management level (How do we get the information? How can we organise ourselves to get the information?)
- Individual meaning level (How do you feel about this conclusion? What is your opinion in this regard?)For example, in the example discussed in the syntax of the model, you should say the problem is experimental in nature and the factors involved in it are sunlight, chlorophyll, carbon dioxide and water. In conducting the experiment, each one should be directed to do a specific activity in the experiment. For those who feel difficulty to internalise the knowledge emerging through the inquiry, you should help them by asking probing questions and comments such as "What is your opinion about 'sunlight is essential for photosynthesis'?" "Wind was not having any effect on photosynthesis", "Temperature does not have any effect on photosynthesis", etc. You should also ask stimulating questions till the student is able to internalise the meaning completely.

Support System

The support system of this model requires a good environment for learning and investigation in the form of a well organised laboratory and a good library. Apart from these, the students should be given support from other media and resources also.

Application of the Model

You can use this model of teaching in traditional classrooms also. Through this model, students will get an opportunity for social interaction, decision making and independent inquiry. You can use a wide variety of problem areas ranging from simple to complex for this method and also for different age levels.

Effects of the Model

This model helps us to foster disciplined inquiry with all age levels. This is also helpful in promoting group work. This model of teaching is considered as very efficient for teaching academic knowledge. This model helps to promote interpersonal interaction, and respect for individuals. This also fosters social inquiry and independence of the learner.

Summing Up

We have discussed the details of group investigation model of teaching. Group investigation means inquiry of a problem by a group. The basic concepts of group investigation are: (i) inquiry, (ii) knowledge, and (iii) dynamics of the learning group.

The model of teaching has syntax, social system, principles of reaction and support system. The syntax has six phases: Phase I is confrontation of puzzling situation, Phase II is exploration of reactions, Phase III is formulation of structuring of the problem, Phase IV is independent and group study, Phase V is analysis of progress and process, and Phase VI is recycle activity.

The status of student and teacher is similar in this model of teaching. Teacher is a facilitator, counsellor and consultant. A good environment for learning and investigation is required for the success of this model. Students will get opportunities to social interaction, decision making and independent inquiry through this model of teaching. It also promotes interpersonal interaction and respect for individuals.

Chapter 13
Mastery Learning

Mastery learning is not a model of teaching, but it is an approach for organising instruction. The proponents of this approach are John B. Carroll and Benjamin S. Bloom. Mastery learning provides an ample opportunity for more students to attain a satisfactory level of performance in school subjects. According to Carroll, learning is directly dependent on learner's aptitude. *The concept of 'aptitude' is the amount of the time required to learn a material.* On the basis of this concept Bloom and Caroll developed a strategy to organise the classroom in such a way that the students will get optimum time, good instruction and assistance in understanding learning tasks. So, as a teacher you should understand the basic concepts of mastery learning and its implications to classroom learning. You should also understand, how to develop mastery learning strategy for classroom instruction. Details of the above mentioned ideas are given below.

Mastery Learning Strategy

We have discussed five teaching models so far. From those models, mastery learning has many differences. It does not appear as a model of teaching, but it is an approach for organising instruction. As it is different from other teaching models, there will not be any typical format of a teaching model in mastery learning. Instead of that, there are some important steps. Before we pass on to the details of the mastery learning strategy, let us see the meaning and basic concepts of mastery learning.

Meaning

You are very much familiar with learning. But mastery learning will be a new term for you. You might have experience in teaching at secondary schools, so you can remember that some of your students were able to learn quickly almost all aspects of the learning material. We usually conduct our classes for such fast learners. When they get mastery over the given material, we proceed to the next task without considering the majority. Mastery learning means learning almost all aspects of a learning material completely within a time span which is different from individual to individual. Now it is clear that the amount of time taken for mastery over a material is different from individual to individual.

Concept of Aptitude

We have already seen that time taken for mastery over a material is different for different persons. So *mastery learning can be referred to as a function of time*. According to John Carroll, the aptitude of the learner is directly linked to learning. Since aptitude is essential for learning, the difference in time required for masterly learning is due to the difference in aptitude. Carrol defines aptitude as, *"the amount of time required for learning the given material"*. If one student is required to master over a material, he should spend enough time which is actually required for getting mastery over that material. This is the basic concept of mastery learning.

Teaching Strategy

The teaching strategy for mastery learning highlights the following aspects such as time allowed for learning, learner's perseverance, the quality of instruction, student's ability to understand instruction, and aptitude.

Aspects of Teaching Strategy

We have already discussed the importance of time allotted for mastery learning. From your own experience it is clear that different individuals need difference in time to learn given material. So, if you want all of your learners to master the given material, you should give enough time to them.

The second aspect is learner's perseverance. Here *perseverance stands for learner's willingness till the successful completion of a task despite of difficulties, his/her attitude towards learning and persistence of motivation*. If the learner does not have willingness to spent enough time for learning s/he could not master over the material. From your own experience you might have noticed that students without interest for learning would be poor learners.

Quality of instruction is the next aspect which influences mastery learning. Quality of instruction is influenced by factors such as competence of the teacher, efficiency of learning situations, variety of learning experiences and mental level of learners. If your instruction takes care of all these aspects, then it will be of good quality.

Student's ability to understand instruction is the next aspect of mastery learning. If your students are not able to understand what is being instructed to them, they could not learn the material and would not get mastery over the material. For example, elementary school children will not have the ability to understand the structure of DNA.

The final and most important aspect of mastery learning is learner's aptitude. We have already discussed the details of aptitude and defined it as the time required for learning.

Steps in Mastery Learning

Mastery learning has five major steps. These are put forth by Bloom.

1. *Formulation of Objectives:* You are familiar with objectives of the lesson from your B.Ed. Training. For any lesson, there will be a list of pre-stated objectives, which determine the purpose of the lesson. The purpose of the learning unit in terms of objectives should be formulated at first.For example, you are going to teach a lesson on food chain. Then you will prepare a set of objectives. (Details of objectives are given in Unit 6.)
   You shall prepare the following objectives.
   The student will be able to:
   a. recall the important terms such as procedures, consumers, decomposers and trophic level;
   b. recognise the difference between different trophic levels;
   c. interpret plants as producers and animals as consumers;
   d. classify organisms on the basis of feeding habits;
   e. apply the information to new situation;
   f. develop scientific appreciation, etc.
2. *Dividing learning units to small units:* Now, we have stated the objectives of the lesson in behavioural terms. You should arrange the learning material into small, short sections. Each small section deals with a single objective, so for the mastery of the material one should master each of these small steps or sections.
   For example, the lesson on food chain can be divided into small sections such as producers, consumers, decomposers, trophic levels and feeding habits.
3. *Identification oflearning materials and instructional strategy:* At this step, you (teacher) should identify the learning materials necessary for the instruction. Then you should select the instructional strategy to master the learning task. For example, the learning materials such as charts, models, and real objects, can be the materials selected. Once you determine the learning material, you should select the suitable instructional strategies. Here you should adopt survey type strategy or lecture cum discussion strategy to teach the lesson on food chain. The design of the proposed instructional strategy should be then practised in the classroom.
4. *Diagnostic Tests:* We have already determined the strategies of instruction. Each unit of the content is accompanied by a brief diagnostic test. These tests are used to measure students' progress in learning and also to identify the particular problems faced by each student. These tests help to know whether each student is able to attain the satisfactory level of performance. Some students might

have certain difficulties in attaining the desired level of performance. So, this test will help us to locate the actual difficulty of the students.

5. *Supplementary Instruction:* We will get the data about the progress of each student and their weak points or difficulties by administering diagnostic tests. You should analyse the data obtained, and provide necessary supplementary instruction or remedial teaching in order to help the students to overcome their difficulties and to attain mastery learning.

You should take care to give enough time to individual students to fit to the aptitude of each student.

Illustration of Mastery Learning

We should know one thing that we can easily implement mastery learning in the usual classrooms, if we are well prepared to understand our students and provide enough time for learning to each of them. Special learning materials such as multimedia packages, programmed learning materials, etc. are very much useful in mastery learning.

An illustration of mastery learning in the form of a self instructional unit is given as follows.

Illustration: A self learning unit developed on the topic 'Food and Health' is given below as an illustration for mastery learning model of teaching.

Food and Health

I. Objectives of the unit

At the completion of this unit the student will be able to:

1. identify different components of food.
2. distinguish between body building components and energy giving components in food.
3. identify resources of different components of food.
4. use of principles of balanced diet in daily life.
5. develop a positive attitude towards balanced diet.
6. identify the importance of vitamins and minerals in diet.
7. develop a positive attitude towards avoiding hyper vitaminosis.

II. Outline of the content

1 Food resources
  1.1 Importance of food
  1.2 Different components of food

2 Balanced diet
   2.1 Meaning of balanced diet
   2.2 Factors influencing the quantity of food needed
   2.3 Importance of balanced diet
3 Malnutrition and hyper vitaminosis
   3.1 Effects of malnutrition
   3.2 Hyper vitaminosis
4 Let us sum up

III. Instructional strategy and learning materials

Instruction of given unit is attempted through self learning materials. Necessary learning materials developed for the learning of the content are listed above for realising the objectives.

Food resources

Food resources are those materials which are used as our food. You are familiar with a variety of food resources. So write down some food resources.

You may have listed out resources such as rice, wheat, fruit, tubers, milk, egg, fish, meat, etc. Among these resources, you shall identify two types on the basis of their origin. That is, vegetarian and non vegetarian food resources. So, we depend upon vegetarian and non vegetarian food items. Now, we shall see the importance of food.

Importance of food

We are usually taking food three or four times a day. What is the importance of food? Food helps us to drive away hunger. What is the use of food? Food gives us energy for our work. Moreover, food helps us build our body and promotes growth. Are the components that give us energy and build our body the same? Now letus see the components in our food.

Different components in food

There are different components in our food. Among them there are energy giving components and body building components. In addition to these components, vitamins and minerals also should be the essential components in food. We shall see each of these components in detail.

Energy giving components

The energy giving components in our food are carbohydrates, fats and lipids. Carbohydrates are different sugars contained in different food resources such as rice, tubers, milk, etc. Fats and lipids are oil content that we get from different food resources such as milk, meat, oils, etc.

Body building components

Proteins, vitamins and minerals are the body building components in our food. Proteins are bigger molecules used for building body parts, that is, cells and cell organelles. We get enough proteins from cereals, beans, milk etc.

Vitamins are vital elements needed for proper growth and functioning of our body. Leaves, vegetables, fruits, fish, egg, milk, etc. are rich resources of vitamins. Minerals are elements which are needed in small amounts for the proper development and functioning of our body. As in the case of vitamins, minerals are also seen in abundance in leaves, vegetables, fruits, fish, egg and milk.

Now we have seen the different components of our food. So, before you proceed to the next section, please answer the following question.

Now we shall pass on to the next section namely, balanced diet.

Balanced Diet

Diet, is the food we take at a time. We are going to discuss in detail the concept of balanced diet, factors influencing the quantity of food a person needs per day and the importance of balanced diet for a healthy life. First of all we shall discuss the concept of balanced diet.

Concept of Balanced Diet

Common balance is a familiar instrument use to measure weight. Suppose, you go to a shop and ask for two kilograms of rice. How do you know that the shopkeeper gives you the same quantity as you demanded? You might be eagerly looking at the balance to see whether the amount of rice taken is well balanced with a two kilogram iron piece. Here the amount of rice taken should be of the same weight that we put in the other side. In the case of diet also, the quantity as well as the quality of food materials we are taking daily should be well balanced with our bodily needs. The quality of food can be determined in terms of the nutrients contained in it. So, we can define balanced diet as the diet which involves all necessary components for the healthy growth of our body in adequate quantity and proportion.

Various components in our food are already discussed in earlier section. The quantity and proportion of each food item is determined by several features which we shall discuss as follows.

Factors influencing the quantity of food a person needs

You might have known some of the factors influencing the quantity of food a person need daily.

You might have the opinion that age of a person and body size are the factors influencing the quantity of food s/he needs daily. Of course, the age and body size are two of such factors. In addition to these, factors such as gender, bodily conditions, climate and vocation also influence the quantity of food one needs daily. We will see each of these factors in detail as follows.

a) **Age:** Requirement of nutrients is different from person to person with difference of age. We know that babies and aged persons need small quantities of food, but with rich nutrients and easily digestible. Otherwise, they might have indigestion problems.
b) **Body size:** A large sized body demands more food than normal body to maintain the functions of the body.
c) **Gender:** Quantity of food one needs is determined by gender of the individual also. Usually men eat more than women. But due to certain physiological conditions such as menstruation, pregnancy and breast feeding woman needs highly nutritious food in more quantities than that of a normal woman and during these conditions extra amounts of nutrients are necessary
d) **Climatic conditions:** Do you ever notice the relationship between climate and our food intake? Of course, there exists a relationship between the two. You may have felt that you need more food in winter season than that in summer season. What will be the reason for this? You might have studied that extra energy is required to maintain our body temperature during winter. That is why we have to take more food in winter.
e) **Vocation:** You may know that the amount of energy one needs is directly related to his vocation. That is, for example, a shopkeeper and a carpenter need different amounts of energy. Because the latter needs more energy for work.

Importance of Balanced Diet

We have discussed the factors influencing quantity of food required for different persons. So, one can determine the quantity and quality of one's own food on the basis of these factors influencing food intake. What will happen if you do not give attention to the quantity of our food intake?

There will be two possibilities: either malnutrition or hyper vitaminosis and obesity. Both of these conditions will lead to different diseases. So it is essential to practise a balanced diet for a healthy life.

Malnutrition

We have seen that different nutrients are required for necessary growth and development of our body and functioning of body systems. If the nutrients are in inadequate amount in food, it would affect the proper functioning of our body and body systems. So, malnutrition is the condition in which the amount of nutrients required for our bodily needs are not obtained through our food. This condition will lead to ill health.

Hyper Vitaminosis

Hyper vitaminosis is the condition which is opposite to the malnutrition. The abundance of various food components in our food will lead to deposition of fats and other minerals at different parts of the body. So, this will lead to obesity. Obesity in turn causes fat deposition inside the blood vessels and at diferent body parts. This will lead to high blood pressure, heart diseases and some other diseases. So, it is also essential to control our diet, for not to increase the nutritious value of food above the required level. Routine exercises also will help us to eliminate the lethal effects of hyper vitaminosis.

IV. Diagnostic Test

The learning material on food and health is given above. You should give the material to your students and allow them to learn till each of them gets mastery over the material. Once they had completed learning of the unit, you should fix the criteria for successful completion as eighty per cent or more marks in the test. You should give supplementary instruction to those who have not successfully completed the unit. (The details of preparing diagnostic test are given in Unit 6). However a sample test question paper is given as follows.

Question Paper

Chapter: Food and Health — Duration: 40 minutes
Standard IX — Marks: 20

I. Fill in the blanks using appropriate word or words **(½x4=2)**

1. Food gives us ....
2. Energy giving components of food are ....
3. Body building components in food are ....
4. Deficiency of nutrient is ....

II. Write your answer in one or two sentences **(1x5=5)**

5. What is Hyper vitaminosis?
6. What is the importance of food in our life?

7. What are the factors influencing the quantity of food needed a day?
8. What is balanced diet?
9. What are the effects of malnutrition?

III. Give your answer in three or four sentences **2x5=10)**

10. In which condition women need more nutrients? Why?
11. How does hyper vitaminosis lead to different diseases?
12. Why do we eat more during winter?
13. Balanced diet is important for a healthy life. Why?
14. Malnutrition and hyper vitaminosis are the two sides of the same coin. Explain?

IV. Answer in 100 words

15. You are going to prepare a balanced diet schedule for your family. What all factors should you take into consideration? Which resources should you include in the diet? Explain **(3x1=3)**

This is only a sample question paper. You should prepare many test items to test each element discussed in the learning unit. Then only you should know whether your students get mastery or not. After evaluating the answer sheet of students, you might have seen that most of them have acquired mastery over the material. If there is anybody who does not get mastery, you will give them supplementary instruction. So, those students will also acquire mastery over the learning unit.

V. Supplementary Instruction

In order to conduct supplementary instruction, you should use the same unit along with some accessory learning materials such as charts, photographs, articles, and talks.

Charts showing different food resources and quantity of food required to each should be used.

You should collect photographs and details of people suffering from diseases due to malnutrition and obesity.

Along with these supplementary learning materials, you should give explanation of the essential aspects of the unit also. Then again conduct a test on the same unit and verify whether all students get mastery over the unit. If needed, you should use some more additional instruction.

Summing Up

In this unit we have discussed in detail the mastery learning strategy of teaching for mastery learning in almost all aspects of a material with a time span which is different from individual to individual. The basic concept of mastery learning is the concept of aptitude. Aptitude is the amount of time required for learning all aspects of a material. Mastery learning strategy has the following aspects, such as time allowed for learning, learner's perseverance, quality of instruction, learner's ability to understand instruction and aptitude. The steps in mastery learning also are discussed.

They are:

- formulation of objectives,
- dividing learning unit into small steps,
- identification of learning material and instructional strategy,
- diagnostic testing, and
- supplementary instruction.

UNIT 5

Media and Materials for Teaching Science

Chapter 14
Laboratory

Everyone who has interest in science teaching would agree that laboratory has immense role in science teaching. Teaching through laboratory or teaching using a laboratory is essential for good science teaching. As a science teacher, we should know the major aspects of a science lab.

Aims and Objectives of Science Laboratory

Laboratory work is essential for complete and meaningful learning of theoretical lessons. So, the theory and practicals act as complementary to each other. The need of laboratory work, you (teacher) should develop details of the plan for the proper utilisation of laboratory facilities.

Through laboratory work we aim to facilitate learning by doing, learning by observation, discovery learning and group investigation approach to learning. For example, you are going to teach differences between animal cells and plant cells. So you should provide slides of the cells and direct your students to observe them using microscope and note the difference between them. This is a mode of discovery learning. Such learning results in better retention for long period of time and also helps to mastery learning. So, maximising learning is the aim of laboratory in science teaching.

Among the objectives of laboratory work, the following are also important.

First objective is to provide concrete experiences for scientific understanding. Let us see an example. Cell division is an abstract idea for students, hours long lecturing may not be helpful in conceptualising the idea. So, instead of lecturing you can utilise lab facilities. Cell division can be visualised using a microscope. Growing roots of onion can be used for this purpose.

Second objective of laboratory is to develop scientific concepts and principles. For example, the concept of factors controlling photosynthesis can be effectively developed with the help of laboratory facilities only.

Scientific skills, scientific attitude, and interest shall be developed through laboratory work. The specific nature of laboratory work would be helpful to develop observation skill, analysing skill, and skill in judgement.

Laboratory is a place for learning scientific method and thus the process of science, i.e. active experimentation and verification. Laboratory work is also helpful to arouse curiosity in scientific phenomena, which in turn inspires learning of science.

Besides these objectives, you can list out many minor objectives of your own for instructional purpose.

Science Laboratory — Features

Usually, majority of us do not give much time for arranging the laboratory. This may be due to many reasons. Such as lack of enough time, lack of enough space, lack of co-operation from others, etc. Still many of us are interested to use the laboratory in maximum possible ways and situations. So, we should know the features of a science laboratory which are as under.

a) A good laboratory should have enough space for the free movement of pupils during laboratory work.
b) The physical conditions such as fresh air, light and ventilation should be adequate to give a conducive environment for laboratory work.
c) The arrangement of the lab should be appropriate to conduct demonstrations, lecture cum demonstrations, individual and group work. You have to demonstrate along with lecturing. Enough facilities should be given for pupils to observe the demonstration and follow it by their individual work.
d) Learning materials such as actual specimens, preserved specimens and materials required for learning should be provided in a science lab.
e) Accessory learning materials such as black board, wall charts, visual aids and display board should be presented in the lab. This would be helpful to maximise the efficiency of instruction.
f) The lab should be designed in such a way to facilitate teacher supervision, it is essential to supervise each student, while they are engaged in practical work.
g) Enough storage facilities should be provided to store lab equipment, accessory learning materials and chemicals.
h) There must have enough water, gas and electric connections wherever it is necessary. Sufficient number of taps and sinks and proper drainage facilities ensure the cleanliness of the laboratory. And there should be proper facilities for waste disposal also.
i) Different types of experiments have to be done in a laboratory using chemicals. So, there must be precautions against any harmful situation in a laboratory. Hence, safety measures such as fire extinguisher, emergency exit, first aid kit, etc. should be provided in a science lab and necessary training for staff and students to handle such situations also is very essential.

Designing Science Laboratory

The science laboratory should be designed in such a way so to consider all the factors related to instruction. Thorough planning in providing any educational situation is important. Here also teacher should plan thoroughly for designing a science laboratory. Before we pass on to the actual design, let us have a look at the important factors, which should be considered at the time of designing a lab.

Factors Influencing the Design of Science Lab

There are various factors which influence the design of science lab. Let us examine them one by one.

a) *Area* – The first one is the number of pupils working at a time. This would help to determine the actual space required for the work area. The space for demonstration and storage should be considered while determining the total area of the laboratory.
b) *Location* – Location of the lab is the second factor which is to be considered at the time of design. It is preferable to locate the lab at the ground floor. The lab should be in such a place where it ensures easy utilisation and access. In our schools, sharing of space and equipments is required. So, lab should be located at a convenient place.
c) *Flexibility* – We use flexibility here to denote the facilities for adopting various activities such as different methods of teaching, activities of science club, facilities for audio-visual projection, space to develop improved learning materials, etc. So you should plan for a multipurpose laboratory.
d) *Furniture* – Necessary furniture such as demonstration table, student tables, storage shelves and chairs are essential in a lab. The tables should not be of huge size. Moderate type table should be preferable. The demonstration table should be placed on adequate height from the ground level, so that the students should be able to see the demonstration well.
e) *Lighting* – Enough lighting should be provided by utilising the daylight to the maximum extent. In order to utilise daylight, doors and windows should be placed in accordance with the entry of light. But care should be taken to avoid excessive lighting. Light colours should be used to paint the walls, which reduces the intensity of light.
f) *Safety* – It is very important to involve safety measures in a science lab. There can be chances of fire, breakable glass wares and harmful chemicals in a lab. So while developing a design for a lab, safety measures must be included in it.

Design of a Science Lab

We have already discussed objectives of laboratories and factors influencing the design of a laboratory. Now, let us develop a design for a model science lab.

The science laboratory in a secondary school might be a multipurpose study room, rather than a laboratory. If there are no separate laboratories for physics, chemistry and biology, we have to share the facilities and utilise it as per the needs of the subject.

Components of a Science Lab

a) *Rooms* – The rooms selected for the laboratory is the first component. The room should have about seventy square metres of space for 40 students. In connection with this room, two small rooms should also be provided at either side of the lab room. The room behind the lab should be used as a store cum preparation room. The room at the other end of the lab should be used as a science museum. The actual laboratory room should have a demonstration area and a work area: the former for conducting demonstration by the teacher and the latter for the student to work.

b) *Storage shelves* – There must be enough storage shelves for the purpose of storing chemicals and other equipment. Most of such shelves should be placed in the store room.

c) *Ventilation* – Enough ventilation should be provided for the lab as we have to use different types of chemicals in lab.

d) *Lighting* – Enough lighting facilities should be provided in the lab. Windows with suitable size should be fixed at appropriate places for this purpose, so as to capture maximum natural light get into the lab. Electrification also should be done to arrange lighting facilities in the lab.

e) *Equipment* – It is essential for every laboratory to have a variety of equipment. The equipment includes dissection microscope, compound microscope, projection microscope and different types of film projectors. Other types of equipment which are necessary for conducting practical in physics and chemistry should also be provided in the lab.

f) *Water connection* – It is very essential for a laboratory to have water connection and sink at appropriate places. A sink should be attached with the demonstration table. Along with the water connection, enough drainage facilities should be provided.

g) *Waste disposal* – There can be different kinds of wastes produced as a result of practical work in science laboratory. Used up chemicals, broken glass wares, biological wastes after dissection, etc. Hence, there must be adequate facilities for the proper treatment of those waste materials.

Safety Precautions in a Science Laboratory

We know that accidents may take place at any time in a laboratory. So, it is very essential to involve certain precautions in a science lab. Let us see the major precautions to be practised in a science lab.

a) *Training for students*: Children are always children. So, they may be exposed to dangerous situations while they are in the lab. It is essential to give necessary training for students in dealing with various equipment. Instructions to operate each equipment should be given properly. Such instructions should be printed and attached with each instrument. You might have noticed such instructions on the equipment that we use. Other instructions for handling chemicals, glasswares, etc. should be exhibited on the walls of the lab and on tables. For example, instructions like "Handle with care" should be pasted on the storage shelves and practical table, which is found very effective. Instructions such as "Keep your table clean", "Chemicals are costly, use them vigilantly", "Prevent fire", "Water is precious", etc. also should be helpful to maintain discipline in the lab. Such steps should be helpful to reduce accidents in the lab. There should be special disaster training for staff and students to deal emergency situations effectively.

b) *First aid kit and training*: Every school should have first aid kits, since injuries are common. We should keep a separate first aid kit in the lab, as it is an accident prone zone. The first aid kit should include cotton, plaster, dressing cloth, medicines to treat injury and burns, and medicine which reduces the chemical action of strong acids. The kit should be kept in such a place, so that everyone could see it and able to use it as and when required. Necessary first aid training should be given to students. This would be helpful to reduce anxiety in the event of any accident.

c) *'Keep-safety' principle:* Many chemicals and objects are dangerous to pupils. So we do not allow them to play with such harmful objects. The list of such injurious things should be a longer one in a science lab. So, you should make a list of objects which are to be kept away from students. Separate list is preferable for chemicals, glass wares and instruments. After making the list you should keep all those objects safely under your custody.

d) *Control Unit*: We use control unit here to denote the on-off and regulation units of electricity and water connection. This unit should be fixed in a convenient corner. You should let the students know the master on and off switches. This would be helpful in the event of accidents, if any. Along with such a unit, proper fuses and earthing of the electrical appliances should be fixed properly.

e) *Emergency Exit*: We are usually unwilling to fix many exits to classrooms, but at the time of an accident only we might feel that the exit is not enough. Thus, it is highly essential to have emergency exits at the places where pupils assemble, especially when it is indoors. Otherwise, the struggle to get out from the accident site itself causes accidents. So, one or two emergency exits should be provided while designing the laboratory.
f) *Fire extinguisher*: A science lab should have facilities to prevent fire. Usually fire extinguisher or sand or water sources are used to prevent fire. It is essential to provide facilities for prevention of fire in a science lab. These are the various safety measures which should be taken into consideration, while we design a science lab.

Management of Science Laboratory

Better management leads to better result. As a science teacher what activities do you follow for the better maintenance of a science lab?

You may suggest that routine cleaning, arrangement of items in the lab, etc. will be helpful for better management. Of course, routine cleaning of the equipment and lab room is essential for better management. Logical arrangement of specimens, equipment and chemicals also surely contribute to the proper management of science lab.

Co-operation of other teachers and students is also helpful to maintain a lab. You should seek co-operation of other teachers and students in collection, preservation, arrangement and storage of specimen and conducting experiments in the lab.

You should entrust members of science club for the better maintenance of the lab. In addition to these, various documents are also essential for maintaining a science lab. Documents such as stock register, purchase register, alphabetical list of equipment, specimens and chemicals and a register to record activities in a lab are also necessary.

We all know that lab is designed for providing practical experience. So, regular use of lab facilities is the most important aspect which contributes to the maintenance of a science lab.

Summing Up

We discussed various aspects of science laboratory. The main points are as follows.

a) Science lab is useful in developing scientific abilities, attitude and interest.
b) The essential physical facilities for a science lab are space, lighting, electrification, and water connection.

c) The factors influencing designing of a science lab are area, location, flexibility, furniture, lighting and safety.

d) The essential components of a science lab are rooms, storage shelves, ventilation, lighting equipment, waste management and water connection.

e) A variety of safety precautions are to be practised such as training for students, first aid kits, control unit, emergency exit, fire extinguisher and keep safely principle.

f) Various activities such as routine cleaning, neat arrangement, co-operation with other teachers and science club members, maintaining records and regular use of the lab, help the proper management of a science lab.

Chapter 15
Learning Aids

Teachers are aware of the use of different types of learning aids from the very beginning of their experience with the career. Learning aids are essential for effective learning. The learning aids are mainly classified into audio, visual and audio-visual aids. In this chapter we shall discuss learning aids in detail.

During instruction, we use many materials and resources to facilitate the process. It may range from a piece of paper to highly sophisticated equipment like computers. Whatever it is, there is no controversy over the fact that these materials are essential for complete and meaningful learning. What do we call such materials?

Concept

The materials and resources which are used to enhance the process of instruction is referred to as learning aids. There are different types of learning aids.

Types of Learning Aids

Learning aids are of a wide variety, but as far as our schools are concerned all of them are not relevant. So, here we will discuss only those which are relevant and available in our schools.

Selected Learning Aids

Visual Aids	*Auditory Aids*	*Audiovisual Aids*
A: Non-projected aids 1. Actual materials 2. Pictorial 3. Mobile chart B: Projected Aids a. Overhead projector b. Film strip/ slide projector	a. Radio b. Record & Record players	1. Cine-sound film & projector 2. Video cassettes/ VCDs 3. Television 4. Computer & mobile phone

From the figure 6 it is clear that there are three categories of learning aids such as visual aids, auditory aids and audio visual aids. Now let us see each one in detail.

Visual Aids

Visual aids are those materials which we can see. A flower, its diagram, or photograph or slide, or transparency, will be a visual aid. Among the visual aids there exist two categories such as non projected aids and projected aids. We know that it is not practical to project a paper chart to a screen. If we need to make an image of an object, we will use slides, films or transparencies. These could be projected using light. So the visual aids which can be projected are called projected visual aids and those cannot be projected are non projected visual aids.

A. Non Projected Aids

These include actual materials, chalk board, charts and mobile charts. When we compare a non projected aid with a projected aid, we can easily understand the advantage of a non projected aid. Non projected aids are more common and widely used in educational practice as it is easy to use without any support of a device. Is there any need for explaining the importance of a chalk board? Because all of us use it extensively. Chalk board can be used at once and at the same time it helps to present new ideas and also for revision and summing up of the lesson. The matter presented on the chalk board can be in verbal, pictorial, or diagrammatic form.

1. *Actual materials*: Actual materials include specimens either in live condition or preserved specimens. As a teacher, you might have used varieties of specimens which are easily available. If such actual materials are not available or difficult to bring into the class, we should utilise other type of aids.
2. *Pictorial aids:* Pictures of various types are used for classroom instruction. They are the second important type of visual aids. The pictorial aids include charts and pictures which serve as valuable visual aids. We can have a wide variety of charts. For example, we can prepare charts for each lesson. As for the chapter 'Our Environment' we can use charts showing animal interactions, food chain, energy flow, pollution, energy ladder and pyramid of energy. Such pictorial presentation will be helpful in facilitating learning. Along with charts, still pictures and photographs are also used as pictorial aids. These will help in understanding seasonal changes and natural phenomenon. For example, the photographs of a particular locality during different seasons, would be helpful to identify the changes occurring in different seasons.

3. *Mobile chart***:** A mobile is a wall chart, but different to natural charts. The difference is in respect of the organisation. There are no pictures, instead of that, symbols or words are arranged independently and hanging separately on threads, on which they can move freely. So they are termed as mobiles.

B. Projected Aids

You might have some experience with projected aids. Mainly three types of projected aids are supplied in our schools. They are overhead projector, slide projector and LCD projector, which is now common. In projected aids, a bright light passes through a transparent picture and by means of a lens the enlarged picture is projected onto screen. The projected aids are more advantageous than non projected ones, as it attracts more attention of viewers. The major projected aids are described below.

1. *Overhead Projector***:** The overhead projector is used to project large transparency sheets. This helps the teacher to present the matter while facing the class. The transparencies are specially developed for overhead projector. Transparencies of living organisms, and the various aspects of living beings are supplied to our schools. These colourful transparencies reduce the effort of the teacher.
2. *Slide Projector:* The slide projector is very useful device to provide real, life like presentation of the content. A wide range of slides are provided to schools in each subject. For example in biology, the slides on internal organs help a lot in the process of instruction. These create greatest inspiration among children to learn.
3. *LCD Projector:* It is a modern equivalent of slide / overhead projector and enables to project videos and images to a screen or any flat surface. Handle this equipment cautiously, as it should be fixed at some place for projection and necessary power backup facility should be provided. Move the LCD projector after its use once it adequately cool down, otherwise its life will be affected.

Auditory Aids

Aids in this group stimulate our audition. The major auditory aids are radio and tape recorders.

a. *Radio:* Radio is one of the cheapest electronic media which has ample educational importance. Now a days there are special educational broadcast for the benefit of pupils as well as for teachers. As an aid, radio act as a supplementary material. Generally two types of radio lessons are broadcast for the benefit of students. They are enrichment lessons and direct teaching. Some lessons are not directly on the content of text books, but are related to the curriculum, these are enrichment lessons. But some programmes are direct on certain areas in school syllabus and are called direct teaching.

The radio lessons are not a substitute to teacher. So teacher must prepare supplementary notes and materials to help the students for better understanding of the lesson. For the effective utilisation of radio lessons, teachers must be vigilant about the schedule of radio programmes. For example, usually radio lessons for students are broadcast at specific time through regional stations of All India Radio. So, the teacher can direct students to listen to the programme and note down the points, which are not clearly understood. Then a discussion on the lesson in the classroom will be helpful for better understanding. Sometimes radio lessons are used along with other projected aids. This would enhance the efficiency of the lesson.

b. *Record and Record players:* We all are familiar with a wide range of audio records. The popularity ranges from its maximum to film songs and declines slowly to educational audio cassettes and CD/DVDs. The records can be easily reproducible and long lasting. The record player is the device (hardware) used to reproduce the recorded material. Among school subjects, a good number of audio materials seem to be highly effective to get mastery over recitation of poems, etc. in languages. Many teachers now utilise this facility in schools. Unfortunately, the use of audio materials in other subjects is very scarce, even though it has many advantages.

Audio Visual Aids

These aids have both an auditory and visual appeal and are more effective than other types of learning aids. These aids are costly and require skillful handling also. The major audio visual aids, which are useful for our school purpose, are cine sound films, video cassettes/CD/DVD, television and computer.

Cine sound and motion film projector: There is an enormous number of films, which provides resources for education. The film helps to communicate complex ideas easily and directly. Films are also helpful in presenting ideas which otherwise cannot be expressed in the classroom. For example, the life of Antarctica cannot be verbally explained clearly. But a sound film on the life of Antarctica would serve the function very well. The newer developments in technology will help to visualise certain biological process, and phenomena, which are otherwise invisible to human eye. The films can also show certain actions more clearly by slowing down its speed, and also reproduce the events already happened. There are short films on 'our nature' supplied to our school, but more number of films must be developed and supplied to the schools. These films can be exhibited only with the aid of sound motion picture projector. While using the projector, care should be taken in cleaning and operation. The threading should be done as per the threading diagram. The projector should be placed on an immovable table and focusing on the screen should be adjusted before projection. Prevalence of computer and digital projectors replace the traditional complicated machinery to easily usable projectors with high definition clarity images.

Video cassettes and video compact discs: Recently, electronic video cassettes exhibit marked advantage over film systems due to their flexibility in self operation and interaction. The video cassettes are costly but important. Nowadays the digital form of content are available which are easy and cheaper to store and handle. When we consider our school environment, it was not even possible to think of the use of such cassettes due to many financial and technical reasons in our country. Educational video cassettes for the secondary level was limited. Though it is a valuable aid for instruction, the lack of enough cassettes and costly nature of hardware make it difficult to use it in our school system. Recently, video cassettes are replaced by VCDs and DVDs, which store data in digital form with more clarity and easy to use, are contributing much to our instructional strategy. The advent of digital storage of data and new software applications make it possible to store huge amount of multimedia data in a very small space, even in a virtual space such as in cloud, by utilising cloud computing technology.

Television: The role of television in education is similar to that of radio in many respects. But it has the same disadvantages of video cassettes. In addition to that, as it is a transmitted medium, time of transmission may be inconvenient and inflexible. Despite these disadvantages, television acts as a highly effective teaching aid. Educational broadcasts for secondary school pupils are adequate nowadays. The television lesson, if utilised for instruction, should be proceeded with teacher's comments and follow up discussion. The role of television in education is now developed in our country. The Victers channel in Malayalam, and Gyandarshan at national level are remarkable television channels exclusive for educational broadcasts.

Computer and mobile phone: Computer brought forth drastic changes in instruction by utilising a variety of software applications. Even computers are now gradually being replaced by mobile phones, which are easy to handle and capable of sharing educational resources to each learner with great precision. Mobile phones with projectors are also available now. A smart phone with Internet connection will be the best teaching-learning aid of the future.

Improvisation of Learning Aids

We have already discussed a number of learning aids. But most of them are costly equipment. So we need to find out similar types of aids at a relatively lower cost. By improvisation we can develop learning aids using low cost, no cost or easily available materials. For example, you are going to teach about pH value. Usually litmus paper is essential. You can make blue litmus paper, by pasting a hibiscus flower on a white paper. You can change it into red litmus by pouring a few drops of lemon juice on it. Likewise you can develop many learning aids according to your content. You can also develop learning aids which are otherwise not available. You can make improvisation of aids as student's projects i.e., collection of resources for learning aids and their development with the help of your students can be a project in that direction. The following pattern will help you for improvisation of learning aids.

Step 1: Identification of the type of aid
We have discussed pedagogical analysis in Unit 3. While analysing the pedagogy, we shall identify the nature and type of learning aids. For example, you are going to teach cell organelles in eighth standard. There is. of course, a need of models of cell as a whole and of different cell organelles. So, identification of type of aid is the first step.

Step 2: Identification of resources required
You should identify the natural resources required to develop the learning aids. For example, you should make a list of resources, such as old newspaper, clothes, empty match boxes, sticks, leaves and flowers of plants, stones, sand, etc., everything can be included in this list.

Step 3: Development of learning aids
Using the collected materials, you should develop learning aids, as per the need of the given content area. You should make a diagram of the material to be developed. Then using the selected resources develops the aid as per the design prepared earlier.

Effective Utilisation of Learning Aids

You are familiar with the selection of appropriate teaching methods, suitable for achieving the objectives of a lesson, on the basis of the characteristics of your students. Each of such teaching method needs inclusion of certain learning aids. Selection of appropriate learning aids and their effective utilisation is a skilled activity. So, before selecting a particular aid, the teacher must ask himself about the kind of aid, the source of its availability, and its effectiveness. After you have selected an aid, you should be familiar with the aid in all its details. Then you have to prepare a plan about, at what point of the lesson the aid is to be introduced. Usually many aids can be introduced at different points of the same lesson. So, you have to plan separately for each aid. After you have a plan about introducing an aid, you have to direct your students to obtain maximum benefit using that aid. For example, before using a microscope, the teacher should explain how to operate it. Instructions to view through it also should be demonstrated. Then comes the actual process of presentation of the aid. The presentation should be as good as possible. Certain aids need follow up discussion after presentation. For example, the students are directed to look at the slide of human blood through a microscope. Once the presentation is over, a discussion on the material will enable to develop a better understanding of the material. As a teacher you have to follow the directions given above for effective utilisation of learning aids.

Summing Up

We have discussed the major types of learning aids, the advantages of each, improvisation of learning aids and means for effective utilisation of learning aids. The main points of the discussion can be summarised as follows.

1. The learning aids can be categorised into visual aids, auditory aids and audio visual aids.
2. Visual aids involve non projected aids such as pictorials and mobile charts and projected aids such as film strip projector overhead projector and LCD projector.
3. Auditory aids involve record and record players, and radio.
4. Audio visual aids involve cine projector, video cassettes, VCD / DVD, television, computer and mobile phones.
5. Improvisation of learning aids is of low cost aids which invites student's active participation.
6. A detailed plan about the type of aid, when to use, how to use and purpose of using will help us in effective utilisation of learning aids.

CHAPTER 16

Accessory Learning Aids

Usually we are using different types of learning aids. We have discussed the major types of learning aids in the last chapter. Now, we shall discuss yet another type of learning aids namely, accessory learning aids. Accessory learning aids involve those aids which can be used for instruction, in addition to the types of aids discussed in earlier chapter. These aids include aids which are used in association with laboratory. Here, we will discuss in detail about accessory learning aids such as museum, aquarium, terrarium and green house.

Meaning

Accessory learning aids mean those aids which could be used effectively for instruction by direct observation from outside the classroom setting. They are permanent setting, usually in association with science laboratory. So, we cannot bring them into the class room, instead you can guide your students for direct observation of different aspects of life and life processes. For example, take the case of aquarium. You should direct your students to observe breathing and feeding habits of fishes, the ecological conditions of aquarium etc.

Science Museum

Museum is an integral part of science instruction. You may have experience regarding the importance of museum in science teaching. Science museum has various purposes. Let us examine the major purposes of science museum.

Purpose of Science Museum

Usually a museum is a place to store and exhibit various types of accessory learning materials. So the purposes of museum are as follows.

a) Collection, storage and exhibition of various specimens, equipment, etc. which have instructional importance.
b) Development of various accessory learning materials such as models, charts, maps, etc.
c) To develop exhibit collection and organisation skill in students.
d) To develop interest in science and helping to sustain the interest.
e) A museum is usually developed as an educational workshop. This can be effected by directing students to take part in various activities.

In addition to these purposes, you may have to suggest some other purposes for science museum. You can try to test purposes of your own. Now, let us discuss about the important inclusions in a museum.

Inclusions in a Science Museum

The items to be included in a museum are as follows. We can collect and preserve any item in the museum, but the materials which have close integration with classroom instruction is preferable. The materials can be dry exhibits such as seeds, leaves, roots, weeds, minerals, etc., and wet specimens such as plants, fishes, snakes, etc. Certain living beings such as birds and large animals should be stuffed and preserved as a part of biology. Different types of equipments used in the past, measuring objects of previous time, models of costly modern equipments, etc. can be included as a part of chemistry and physics.

Models of various materials should be developed and protected in the museum. The models can be still models or working models, could be made using low cost and no cost materials and clay, plaster of paris, sponge, etc. Charts and maps of selected topics also can be prepared.

Usually the museum is seen in connection with the laboratory. Enough shelves should be provided in the museum to arrange all the exhibits systematically. Work tables also should be provided in a museum to prepare different types of accessory learning materials. Now we shall discuss the important aspects of specimen collection and preservation. Preservation is more important for biological specimen.

Specimen — Narcotisation and Preservation

Here we consider the wet specimens. We have already seen that plants, invertebrates and vertebrates can be preserved as wet specimens. And preservation of plants is easier than that of animals. The selected plants should be collected and preserved in a suitable medium. But preservation of animals have two stages, namely 1) narcotisation and 2) preservation. Let us see each one in detail.

A. *Narcotisation of animals*: Narcotisation means killing an animal in an unconscious stage with the application of certain chemicals, which make the animals unconscious and then kill them. Different types of chemicals are used for this purpose. Let us see some of the useful ones.

   1. Menthol: This is helpful to kill invertebrate animals living in aquatic medium. Ten percent (10%) solution of menthol is enough to narcotise and kill an aquatic invertebrate within half an hour.
   2. Magnesium sulphate:This is very effective to narcotise and kill most of the marine and fresh water forms. Selected animals

are to be put in water and add a few crystals of magnesium sulphate. It will gradually dissolve in water, which leads to the narcotisation of animals.

3. Magnesium chloride: This is also a useful chemical for narcotising aquatic forms. For marine animals 7.5% solution of magnesium chloride with an equal part of sea water is useful. And for fresh water forms 2.5% solution is sufficient. Alcohol (20%-50%) also is used for narcotising animals. Chloroform is another narcotic agent used to narcotise terrestrial forms.

B. *Preservation of animals*: You may be familiar with preserved animals. Glass jars with suitable size is necessary for preservation of animals. Appropriate preservative should be added to the glass jar and put the specimen in the jar. Different preservatives are used for preserving animals.

Formaldehyde is a widely used preservative. Commercial formalin should be reduced to 5% solution for preserving most invertebrate animals. For vertebrate formalin of 5-10% is suitable. Ethyl alcohol is another preservative. You can prepare Bovine's fluid a preservative mixture, by adding equal amounts of picric acid, formalin, glacial acetic acid and alcohol.

Herbarium

Herbarium is a very useful method for preserving plant parts in dry condition. Usually a plant twig with inflorescence should be used for this purpose. The selected plant should be dried at first. Now let us see how to press dry the plant parts.

A. *Press drying*: Press drying is a process to dry plant parts for preservation. It is, as the name indicates, drying by pressing. You should take the material to be dried and place it on a sheet of newspaper. Another sheet of paper is to be placed over it and place a pile of books over it to compress the specimen. You can place many specimens with alternate sheets of newspapers in this way. You have to replace the wet newspaper everyday. This will help to complete the drying process without shrinking of any part. If you place a cardboard sheet in between newspaper sections, the drying will be at a faster rate.

You should take certain precautions while placing the specimen for drying. They are as follows.

i) Flattened flowers, if any, should be placed face down on the paper.
ii) Long flowers should be laid for side view.
iii) Cut the stem according to the size of the paper.
iv) Leaves should be spread clearly.

v) If the specimen is wrinkled, before drying it should be soaked in water to get its proper appearance.

These are the points to be borne in mind for press drying a specimen.

B. *Preparation of Herbarium*: This is the second phase, i.e. the preservation phase. Usually we use drawing paper of A4 size for this purpose. After the drying process is over, you should take the specimen for preservation. This specimen is then carefully pasted on the herbarium sheet. Each herbarium sheet should contain only one specimen. And each sheet should have the following details of the specimen: Scientific name, family, locality of plant, local name, date of collection and name of the collector. These details should be neatly written or printed on the right hand side, lower part of a herbarium sheet. Then you should cover the sheet using thin and transparent polythene sheet. These sheets should be filled separately or bind them into a book as per your convenience.

Aquarium

Aquarium has high ornamental value along with its educational significance. Aquarium can also be used to conduct project work for students of different standards. Now, we will discuss the scope of an aquarium.

Scope of Aquarium in Science Teaching

Aquarium has wide scope in teaching even from elementary stage. It helps to make the students active, while they are learning. Since aquarium provides actual life situation, it reduces our work to a greater extent.

You could assign certain problems to students and guide them to solve those problems by thorough observation of aquarium. It is an effective medium to understand the changes in ecosystem as well as effects of various factors in an ecosystem. Aquarium is also a very good device to conduct project work for students of different abilities. For example, the difficulty level of the project can be progressively upgraded from low ability students to students with higher abilities. Many experiments can also be conducted using an aquarium. For example, cyclic nature of elements, feeding habits of different types of animals, food of living things in the aquarium, necessity of the hygiene surrounding, etc. can be experimentally proved using an aquarium. You should design and conduct experiments of your choice using an aquarium.

Construction of Aquarium

We all are familiar with aquarium, but all of us are not so familiar about the construction of an aquarium. The following items are required to set an aquarium.

a) Glass jar — A clear glass jar is the most important part of an aquarium. Usually rectangular glass jars are used for this purpose. Glass jars in many shapes are used now. If separate glass pieces are used to construct the aquarium, the joints should be sealed in such a way to prevent water leakage.
b) Clean sand and stones — The sand should be washed thoroughly many times to eliminate mud particles. Along with sand, attractive stones should be collected and cleaned. These can be used to decorate the floor of the aquarium with a little slope from front side to back side.
c) Aeration facility — You might have seen different sized and shaped aerators used in aquarium. You should select aerators in accordance with the size of the glass jar that you have selected. You should provide electric supply to the aerators, otherwise they will not work.
d) Water plants — You can select some water plants of suitable size to plant in the aquarium. The roots of the plants selected should be washed thoroughly to remove mud particles. Hydrilla and Valisnaria are commonly used plants.
e) Fishes and other water animals — Now your aquarium is ready. And you should select suitably sized fishes for the aquarium. Other animals such as snails also should be reared in the aquarium.
f) Other Equipment — Equipment such as net to catch fishes, equipment to remove polluted water and to provide clean water to the aquarium should be provided.

These are the important components of an aquarium. Now let us see the guidelines for maintaining the aquarium.

Guidelines to Maintain Aquarium

The aquarium should be placed at some height and a position where adequate sunlight and wind can be obtained. Fishes should be fed regularly at a particular time. And water and materials in the aquarium should be changed periodically. You (teacher) should assign the duty of maintenance of the aquarium as an activity of the science club.

Terrarium

Terrarium may be a new term for you. Terrarium is a sealed transparent container used for growing plants. That is, selected plants are growing in sealed, transparent settings. Any type of glass jars can be used for this purpose. But very small containers should be avoided.

In addition to educational purposes, terrarium has decorative value also. We can keep them 'in doors' in this regard. Terrarium will help you for the instruction of soil texture, spacing of plants while planting, influence of humidity, and growth of plants in controlled conditions. Now we shall discuss setting up a terrarium.

Setting a Terrarium

The material required are clean glass jar, gravel / charcoal pieces, soil mixture, sand, moss, plants and tools for planting, watering, and pruning. Soil mixture should contain two parts of fibrous foam soil, two parts sand and one part leaf particles. Take the glass jar and clean it well. Gravel or charcoal pieces should be spread at the bottom of the jar for about an inch thickness. Then take the soil mixture, and make it moist before putting it in the jar. For this purpose, add water in the middle of the soil mixture until it became crumby. Then put the mixture in the jar. Now the terrarium is ready for planting.

Planting and Maintenance

Before planting, we should select the plants suitable for planting. Usually plants such as lichens, selaginella, ferns, and flowering plants such as Begonia and Jasmine are long lasting in terrarium. Then we decide the arrangement of plants in the terrarium.

Once plants are selected the plants, these are to be transferred with soil around its roots for fixing in the terrarium with adequate spacing. Soil should be pressed firm around the sides of the root after fixing them in the terrarium. And then we should cover the jar with plastic or glass cover to maintain humidity inside the terrarium. The amount of humidity is very important as far as the maintenance of terrarium is concerned. Excess humidity should be reduced by opening the cover for the required time. Appearance of small drops of water on the sides of the jar indicates excess humidity in terrarium. If humidity is less then it is to be increased to the desired level by adding adequate water. We should remove dead and decayed vegetation as soon as possible from the terrarium. Pruning should be done to provide enough space for plant growth. If plants are grown weak, fertilisers should be added to the soil by diluting them to one fourth of its concentration. Terrarium should not be placed in full light but only in partial light. If we are successful to maintain all these conditions, the terrarium shall remain intact.

Green House

Green house is a controlled environment in which various plants can be grown. The control is mainly in terms of sunlight and humidity. Since, we have control over the environment, we can grow aside variety of plants throughout the year, i.e., regardless of seasonal climatic changes. We know that the growth of plants is season specific. So, if we can provide such an environment without seasonal changes, we can cultivate plants regardless of seasons. That is the advantage of green house.

Components of a Green House

Components of a Green House means the material required for constructing a green house and its various inclusions. First of all, we shall see the building material required for constructing a green house.

Building material required: All of us know about various material used to construct a building. Similarly, material such as wood, metal pipes, brick or stones are necessary for constructing the basement and the frame of the green house also. Polyethylene sheets can be used to cover the frame of the green house. A blanket is also required to cover the polyethylene covering at times to prevent heat loss from green house when there is extreme cold outside the green house.

Inclusions in a Green House

Inclusions in a green house mean various plants to be grown in the green house. Plants such as ornamental plants, medicinal plants, edible plants, vegetables, small herbs, etc. can be grown effectively in a green house. We know that in order to grow plants, planting pots are necessary. There should be frames or arrangements necessary to place the pots, instruments for planting and watering are also necessary. These are various material and inclusions in a green house. Now let us see how to build a green house.

How to Build a Green House

We can build a Green House either attached with the main building or independent of the building. First of all, we shall see the green house attached to a main building or house.

The green house must face south, i.e. the slope of the roof should be towards south. This will help to get maximum sunlight into the green house. The roof should be made lighter with plastic sheets only or with plastic sheet and glass pane together. You should provide 2.5 to 5 cm air column between them. If a double layer of polyethylene sheet is usee, then it should be replaced by a new sheet in every two years. Ventilation facilities are to be made, while building the green house, this will help to avoid excess heating. Supplemental lighting facility also is essential. We should use fluorescent lamps for this purpose. Now, we shall discuss a green house constructed independent of any building.

An independent green house is easy to build and cheaper than attached type green house. In this type, a semi circular frame is the main component of the green house. This frame should be made of wood or metal pipes. Horizontal support, if necessary, should be provided for polyethylene sheet. Ventilation and lighting facilities should be the same as that of the attached type green house. These are the essential aspects in building a green house.

Instructional Uses of Green House

Before we discus about the instructional uses of green house, being a teacher you should yourself first think about some of the instructional uses of green house.

You might have thought about the following instructional uses for a green house.

i) It helps in studying growth of plants, flowers and uses for a green house.
ii) It helps to study the influence of climate on plant growth.
iii) It also helps to compare different types of plants and their rate of growth.
Along with these some other uses are also there. Let us see the other uses also.
iv) Building and maintenance of green house can be done as a student activity. Thus, it will help to develop a positive attitude towards science.
v) You can direct students to compare the rate of growth of plants inside and outside the green house.
vi) Different types of pollination, need of pollinating agents, artificial pollination, etc. can be easily learned with the help of a green house.
vii) Moreover, green house will be a place for students' group work and can foster scientific attitude and inquiry skills in them.
These are the various instructional uses of a green house.

Summing Up

We have discussed various types of accessory learning aids. The meaning of accessory learning aids and different aids such as a science museum, aquarium, terrarium and green house are discussed in detail. Accessory learning aids mean those which are essential for instruction and which are seen in close association with classroom setting.

Science museum includes different kinds of specimens, both animals and plants. Different techniques for narcotising and preserving specimens are discussed. Procedure for herbarium preparation also is discussed.

The discussion on aquarium involves:

i) Scope of aquarium in science teaching,
ii) Construction of an aquarium, and
iii) Guidelines to maintain an aquarium.

The discussion on terrarium involves:

i) Setting a terrarium, and
ii) Planting and maintenance of a terrarium.

The discussion on a green house involves:

i) Components of a green house,
ii) Details of building a green house, and
iii) Instructional uses of green house.

Chapter 17
Community Resources

Community is a great human laboratory and a very efficient instructional medium. Due to high educational value, people and activities in a community can be used as effective educational resources. Planned interactions with adults of the community would provide new horizons of knowledge for students. Learning about the community as an active member is important for each individual. Learning different social roles and significance of such roles in social productivity could be attained through such participatory study only.

Concept of Community Resources

A community is the gathering of a variety of things, persons, and innumerable interactions and incidents. A community has immense value in terms of resources. We all know that there are variety of resources in a community. Here, we will see community resources which are useful for instruction. For example, a pond has importance in teaching ecosystem, and hence it is considered as a community resource. Likewise, a health visitor who is able to give instructions about health and hygiene to pupils is an important resource in a community. So, such persons are also considered as community resource. Hence, anything in a community which is useful and be able to utilise for instruction is referred to as a community resource. In few occasions, community resources are used for entertainment purpose

Major Community Resources

The community resources can be mainly of two types—material resources and human resources. The material resources include institutions such as zoo, museum, planetarium, libraries, theatre, cultural centres, factories, ponds, lakes, rivers, water falls, etc. come under this category. The human component involves various agencies and personnel. The agencies are —health services, post and telegraph services, teachers' organisations, science organisations, transport services, etc. The resource personnel can be a leader, social worker, a teacher or anyone who is an expert in the corresponding field. For example, a motor mechanic who can explain the various aspects of working and failure of a motor is an important resource. Hence, for a teacher everything in the community has its own utilisation value in the point of view of education.

How to Utilise Community Resources

Use of community resources in science teaching is mainly three-fold. At first, by bringing the resources into the classroom; secondly, by requesting persons to come to school and give lectures; and thirdly, by making arrangements to visit such places of resources. In many of these cases you should be thoroughly prepared to utilise the resources successfully.

Survey of resources: A survey to identify the resources in a community can be conducted with the help of your students. You can identify various types of resources through the survey. Suppose you conduct a survey to identify the resources in your community. You will get a list of resources in your community.

Analysis of resource list: After getting the list, analyse the list to identify the useful ones. Useful ones in the sense that they are useful for teaching of science. The survey might provide the whole list of resources in your locality, so you should analyse the list to identify the usable resources. This analysis should be based on the content area to be instructed in different standards. You have to ask questions such as — Is this resource useful for teaching? If so why? And what are its uses? — in order to analyse each of the resources. You will thus get a list of useful resources from the whole list of resources. Now we shall identify which all resources are accessible to us.

Identification of accessible resources: All the resources from the list of useful resources cannot be used due to practical difficulties. For example, it is better not to visit a factory producing pesticides and fumigants, a risky place (a water fall), etc. A person, though highly qualified, is not able to talk at the level of secondary school learners will not be an accessible resource. So, you should identify the accessible resources on the basis of utilisability of each useful resource. Then a list of useful and realisable resources should be finalised.

Classification of resources: Detailed alphabetical list should be formed for each category of resources. For example, separate lists should be formed for various agencies such as government agencies, private agencies and voluntary agencies. The list should include transport services such as airports, railway station, bus depots and ports; business organisations; and special organisations and places such as planetarium, aquarium, ponds, lakes, etc.

Each list should be on separate sheets, and arranged in such a way, as to facilitate updating of information.

Similarly, a classified list of individuals in the community, who have expertise in their own field, and who are willing to come to schools to share their knowledge, also should be prepared.

If any unusual resources are present in the community, that also should be categorised into a special list. For example, a blood bank, a milk dairy, etc. come under this category.

Data required for utilisation of resources: While preparing the list of resources you should enclose the following necessary data pertaining to the resources. First of all, you should know name of the resources, then you should know location of the resources. For utilising a resource you should know the person to whom contact should be made to get access to the facility; What procedures are there for the utilisation of resources?; Will it serve the purpose?; and Is there any restrictions for its utilisation? Also prepare a map of the place to show the locations of various resources in your community. Formats to obtain permission also should be developed by the teachers to get permission from the concerned authority. In addition to all these, you should develop a detailed plan for linking your lesson with the resource which you plan to utilise for instruction.

Scope of Community Resources in Teaching Science

The common practice in our country has made teaching of science a talk show. We cannot blame the science teachers in this respect. Because the facilities available in school are very limited. And we are not in a position to purchase each and every equipment. Here comes the scope of utilising community resources. There are innumerable facilities for teaching science in our community. The community resources would be helpful in providing direct experience in many instances. For example, pasteurisation techniques can be understood easily by a visit to the nearby dairy farm.

Community resources are helpful in adopting a variety of approaches in teaching. Let us consider an example. You have prepared to teach ecosystem, so you give directions to the students to observe a particular pond in the locality and make a list of plants and animals there. Here, you can conduct a general survey only. You can give directions for group investigations on the following tasks. Identification of the types of green plants (in different groups such as floating, submerged, etc.) and different levels of consumers at different trophic levels. Learning is facilitated by firsthand experience in concrete manner than that of abstract form. For example, you want to teach about amoeba. At first, you may talk about the size of an amoeba using a diagram. Instead of the chart if you use a microscope and slide, it will be more effective to develop the concept of the size of an amoeba.

Observation and problem solving ability can be developed using community resources. They are also helpful in providing firsthand information about natural setup, i.e., within the community system.

So, it is your task to deal effectively with the available resources for instruction as well as to enable the student to see the real world in which they will enter.

Model Schedule to Utilise Community Resources

a) *Area Map*:

An area map of your locality should be developed to understand the location of various resources

b) *Alphabetical list of resources*:

All the resources should be arranged in alphabetical order under separate sub headings.

- Animal farm
  Dairy farm
  Poultry farm
  Any other
- Ecosystem
  Forest land
  Pond
  River
- Factory
  Rubber factory
  Soap factory
  Tile factory
  Any other
- Higher education institutions
  Arts and Science colleges
  Higher secondary schools
  Industrial training centre
  Any other
- Library
  Public library
  Youth club library
  Any other
- Offices
  Panchayat office
  Police station
  Post office
  Village office
  Any other

c) Alphabetical list of personnel

Doctor	*Name and Address*	*Phone no., if any*
Engineer	"	"
Factory manager	"	"
Farmer	"	"
Librarian	"	"
Panchayat officer	"	"
Police officer	"	"
Post master	"	"
Veterinary officer	"	"
Zoo keeper	"	"
(You should develop your own list)		

d) Special list of unusual resources

Aerodrome
Planetariums
Research laboratories
Shipyard
TV station

e) Permission procedure:

You should write the permission letter on the letter pad of your institution

To

....

....

Sub: Educational visit to ....(name of institution) request regarding –

I request you to give permission for a group of students (........... nos) and teachers (........... nos) to visit your institution on a convenient day in the month of .... Please inform us about the date and time allotted to us.

Thanking you, Yours faithfully

Head of Institution

(Some additions can be made according to the change in resources)

f) Transportation facility:

The roads should be marked clearly in the area map. So, the actual distance required to reach the place is determined and necessary arrangements should be done for transportation. You should also plan when to start and when to return, how to spend time at the place of visit, etc.

g) Instructions to students:

The instructions should be appropriate to the place which we propose to visit. Cautionary instructions such as, 'Behave decently', 'Don't touch anything unnecessarily', 'Always keep quiet', etc. can be used. Instructions to attain maximum utility of the resources should also be given.

h) Uses of resources:

You should develop a detailed plan about the uses of resources. For example, you plan to visit a pond along with the students. So, you should plan well in advance for 'how should I teach ecosystem by utilising this resource?' It is better to give necessary directions to the students about the purpose of our journey.

Summing Up

We have analysed various aspects of community resources, in terms of its influence on teaching. The following are the main points emerged from the analysis.

- Community resources is anything that could be useful and realisable for instruction.
- Community resources can be of two types namely material resources and human resources.
- In order to utilise the resources, you should survey the resources at your locality, identify them, classify them, and collect the data about its name, location and educational importance.
- Community resources have wide scope in education as it provides real life situations to your students.
- A schedule for utilising community resources should include an area map, alphabetical list of resources, permission procedure, transportation facility, instruction to students and uses of resources.

Chapter 18
Extended Curricular Activities

Activities outside the curriculum and the activities in accordance with curriculum are very important as far as science teaching is concerned. There, of course, are varieties of such activities. The organisation and execution of such activities demand expert planning on your part. Some of such very essential extended curricular activities, in terms of their aims and organisation are discussed here.

In Education we have three types of activities, commonly called as curricular activities, co-curricular activities and extra-curricular activities.

Meaning

Co-curricular activities are also named as extended curricular activities which are the extensions of the curricular activities. In other words, we have numerous curricular activities and along with it, there can be other activities which should supplement the curricular activities. These activities are termed as extended curricular activities, because they supplement the curricular activities. Moreover, these activities are mainly meant for students having more interest in science. For example, conduct of science projects is an example for an extended curricular activity. Usually science projects are assigned to students who have more abilities, and interest in science. So, such extended curricular activities are helpful to cater to the needs of average and above average children to explore scientific knowledge, to test the relevance of existing knowledge and to apply the knowledge in new situations. The important extended curricular activities with respect to science curriculum are as under.

Important Extended Curricular Activities

The important extended curricular activities in science are Science Club, Science Exhibition, Science Quiz, Field Trip and Science Projects.

Science club helps us to develop scientific awareness among learners and extend many classroom activities to the real situation.

Science exhibitions help us to foster the creative abilities of learners and to promote organisational skill in them. Most of the exhibits can be the extensions of school syllabi.

The rapidly developing nature of science, its recent developments, and newer explorations can be exposed through science quiz. This helps us to gather more advanced and recent knowledge about what we already know.

Fields trips serve as a curricular activity sometimes and it has profound influence in the learning of science. Usually we confine science teaching to classrooms. So, field trips are actual extensions of classroom experience to give direct experience related to science.

You might have been troubled by your gifted students at least once in every class, as they may be getting bored over the meaningless repetitions. In such cases, projects will help you to a great extent. Projects can be used to satisfy the needs of fast learners to test and verify their existing knowledge and to explore new knowledge.

So, all the activities mentioned earlier have a direct bearing on classroom instruction. Each of such activities has profound influence in science teaching.

Science Club

Science club has become an inseparable part of our school system. You might have some experience with regard to science club. The science club has to lead many scientific activities in school. Let us see the aims and objectives of the science club.

Aims of Science Club

Science club is a mediator between classroom teaching and laboratory work. Science club is helpful in many ways such as: to create interest in science, to learn process of science, to understand scientific principles, etc. On the basis of importance of science club the following aims are determined.

a) To develop scientific awareness among students: Various activities should be organised by the science club. These activities enhance students to develop scientific awareness.
b) Understanding the method of scientific research: You can give so many problems in science to students. Solving of many such problems require investigation and research which help to understand the method of scientific research.
c) Development of critical thinking: Critical thinking can be developed only through scientific inquiry, observation and analysis of data.
d) Interest in scientific activities: Since science club invites active involvement of students in a variety of scientific activities, it helps to develop and sustain interest in scientific activities.
e) Identification of career opportunities: Students have to gather information from various sections of the society. It helps the students to identify various career opportunities in our society.

Organising a Science Club

Usually one teacher is selected as a staff representative to organise science club and its activities. You should inform students about the importance of science club. A meeting of the interested students should be conducted at a convenient time. An executive committee should be formed in this meeting. The executive committee under the leadership of a secretary is the organising body of the science club. The meeting time of science club should be fixed in advance. The activities should be generally of four categories, namely lectures and reading, preparation of materials, advanced science projects and preparation for science exhibition. You should request the head of the institution to give some financial assistance for the successful functioning of the science club.

Activities of Science Club

We have organised a science club to keep students active in learning science. So naturally you should plan and execute those activities in which students have interest. There may not be a readymade set of activities and you need not impose your ideas on students. Your role is just to let happen the idea put forth by the students and to prepare necessary guidelines for them. The following are suggested as a model for activities of a science club.

a) Organising lectures, debates and topics for symposium of scientific interest.
b) Collecting articles that have scientific interest and exhibit in the science news board.
c) A survey of the community to realise various community resources.
d) Preparing charts, models and conducting experiments related to classroom learning
e) Conducting project work on various topics related to science.
f) Organising science fair and science exhibitions.

You should select and conduct various other activities according to the interest of your students and the facilities available.

Science Exhibition

Exhibition is the process of exhibiting various items, including projects. The science exhibition has many advantages with respect to science education. It is highly effective in developing various skills such as skill in problem solving, skill in organising and skill in analysing relationships. Exhibitions should also facilitate science learning and develop scientific interest and appreciation. You might have experience in conducting exhibitions successfully. You should also point out some other merits of the science exhibition.

Organisation of Science Exhibition

The organisation of an exhibition is a strenuous activity. Various factors are to be considered while organising an exhibition. Usually in our schools, the conduct of exhibition is the responsibility of the science clubs. Planning is first and most important component of organising an exhinition.

Planning for Science Exhibition

The planning should involve the following components

a) *Area requirement*: You have to plan the total area required to conduct the exhibition. If it is conducted for more than one day, the room or hall selected should have locking facilities.
b) *Beginning time and duration*: You should plan the actual beginning time and duration of the exhibition. It would be helpful for you to make necessary arrangements.
c) *Committee*: You should form different committees of students to facilitate the conduct of exhibition. Committees such as organising committee, planning committee, finance committee, publicity committee, refreshment committee, award committee, and safety committee should be formed.
d) *Judgement and awards*: You should plan for the judgement of best items exhibited in the programme and prize should be given for them. This should be done with the help of award committee. You should take precaution to maximise objectivity in judgement.
e) *Budget*: Financial resource is very essential to conduct the exhibition. You should request the head of the institution for financial assistance. You should ask finance committee to develop the budget.
f) *Publicity:* Publicity committee is responsible for giving wide publicity to the exhibition. You should give necessary guidelines for the students in this regard.
g) *Guidelines*: A group of teachers should be selected to give necessary guidelines to the students in various committees. You should be vigilant to give directions, wherever required.

Guidelines to Conduct Exhibition

Science exhibition is a co-operative activity of all the teachers and students. Other teachers may say that it is the duty of science teachers. But you should seek the co-operation of every teacher to conduct the exhibition. So, you have to bear in mind the following guidelines.

a. *Co-ordination of staff and students*: To make the fair an event, you should co-ordinate all the teachers and the members of students, selected to the various committees.

b. *List of items:* Make a list of all the items to be exhibited. Separate list in different subjects is preferable.
c. *Guidelines to teachers*: Give necessary guidelines to all the teachers regarding their duty. For this purpose, divide and distribute the duties to all the teachers and depute them to various committees.
d. *Guidelines to students*: You should prepare the students who are going to exhibit items in the fair. Necessary directions should be given to arrange the items and how to explain and demonstrate the exhibited items.
e. *Safety precautions:* As dangerous chemicals, equipment and electricity lines are essential in the fair, so take necessary precautions to handle them vigilantly to prevent any mishappening. You should also see that a first aid kit is available in the exhibition hall.
f. *Evaluation*: After the completion of the fair, a general body meeting of all the committees should be organised to evaluate the various aspects of the fair with respect to its success and failure.

Science Quiz

As science teachers, you must have some experience in organising quiz programme in science. Because, we have to select one or two students to participate in sub district level quiz competition. Even then, most of us are unaware of the important aspects of this activity.

Aims of Science Quiz

Quiz is an important extended curricular activity. The major aims of science quiz are as follows.

- To explore new information: While participating in quiz programmes, students will get a chance to acquire advanced and recent information. Usually the questions of a quiz programme comprise of advanced and recent information. This will help students to acquire such valuable information and help to develop scientific awareness.
- To develop interest in scientific activities: Along with quiz programme, many other activities such as science club, science fair, field trip and science projects are the activities of science. Participation in quiz programmes will help students to promote interest in other scientific activities also through which they can gain advanced knowledge.
- To develop communication skill: Development of communication skill is very important, as we have to communicate effectively with other members of the society. Through programmes like quiz we can develop communication skill in children.

  These are the major aims of science quiz.

Organising Science Quiz

Though it seems simple, organisation of quiz programme involves several components or steps as under

i. *Announcement*: The first step of quiz programme is with respect to venue, date and time, theme / topic and whether it is oral / written. Announcement should be given in advance so that students should get enough time for preparation. You should give at least one week's time for preparation. If the programme to be conducted as in written form, you should give necessary directions to your students to bring materials for writing or to distribute it for all the participants.

ii) *Preparation*: At this stage you should collect any number of questions suitable for quiz programme. You should then select questions of appropriate number. Collect the list of participants, and then make necessary seating arrangements for them. The quiz master, preferably a science teacher, should be supportive, communicative and energetic person. If you conduct oral form of quiz, select one teacher as marker in addition to quiz master, who will be in charge for marking scores on the score board.

These things should be done at the preparation stage.

iii) *Conduct of quiz programme*: After completing the preparation and arrangements, you should conduct the programme. Enough seating and lighting facilities should be arranged for participants, quiz master and listeners. The score board should be placed in such a way that it is visible for all at the venue. The questions should be placed in such a way that it is visible for all at the venue. The questions should be asked loudly and should be explained, if necessary. At the end of the programme, tabulation should be done and results should be declared. These are the procedures to be followed while organising science quiz programme.

Field Trips

Field trip may be considered as an active and special kind of laboratory situation. Some field trips demand students to be actively engaged in collecting, observing, evaluating and manipulating items. In this case, it is like a laboratory situation. In other trips, it provides opportunity to observe and gain specific information. Field trips can play a very vital role in teaching biology. This will help the students to learn natural phenomena, to understand basic principles of ecology and its application for better living and conservation, and to develop skills such as collecting, identifying and studying equipment, objects, and specimens. Go through your syllabus to identify the topics to which you can arrange field trips.

Organising a Field Trip

In any organisation, planning is the primary activity. Similarly, in organising a field trip also, planning is the first stage. Planning should have the following activities.

Selection of the place of visit: The selection of the place of visit should be done by the teachers. At the time of selection, distance from school to the place of visit, time required for journey, travelling facilities, time required to visit the place fully, and the richness of the place also should be taken into consideration.

Preparation of outlines: After selecting the place, you should familiarise yourself with the area and be familiar with the resources available at that place. Then the teacher should develop an outline (keys) of that place which helps to prioritise proper utilisation of the visit.

Contact with authorities: The teacher should get advance permission from the authorities to visit the proposed place. This is usually needed at the time of visit to a biological park or industry. It is known to us that without permission we cannot visit such places.

Instructions to the students: Before the actual trip, the teacher should give necessary instructions about how to observe, what to observe and how to differentiate one from the other. The teacher has to give a brief description of the place, which helps the students to adjust easily with the place when you reach there.

Materials to the students: Now let us examine the materials required for studying different science subjects from the place of visit. They are collection of bottles, plastic bags, nets for collecting insects, or adequate specimen. Also magnifying lenses, pen knife, preservatives and first aid kit.

Assignments to students: The teacher should also prepare a set of assignments for different groups of students. This would help to cover up all the details of the place and it helps the teacher to manage the students well. Certain special assignments also should be prepared to those students who have greater interest. It is desirable to give all assignments to all groups, because everybody shall get an idea of all required items.

Follow up work: This is perhaps the tail end of field trip. This is usually done in the form of discussion on the very next day of the field trip. This should help the teacher to evaluate whether the purpose of the trip was accomplished. This follow up discussion is also helpful in better understanding and identifying the shortcomings of the trip.

Science Projects

Project is a very effective method for learning science and scientific methods. In our schools, we use very simple projects for awarding CE marks. Projects for instructional purposes are seldom used in our schools.

A project is defined as a planned undertaking specified for a purpose, and usually involves a task or problem in need of constructive thought and action.

Though project method is used for group investigation, it could be effectively utilised for the individual needs of students, especially of the gifted and highly interested students. You should help your students to conduct project work on the problems which they proposed as doubts. Project work is a prolonged activity, which takes many hours and days for its completion. But, while the students start working on a project, they will get attached to it and will be able to learn the process of science more easily.

Components of Science Project

Project work means some sort of research work. So it must be scientific and systematic. There are a number of components in a project as under.

1. *Background research*: Of course, a learner shall have a number of problems to be selected for the project work. Before finalising the topic, you should conduct background research to find out its nature, characteristics, difficulties and methods to be adopted.
2. *Selection of the topic*: Consider that the learner select the topics as "Sunlight affects photosynthesis". Then you have to ask yourself. Whether it is difficult? Whether all the resources are available? Are there any necessary guidance facilities? Is it valuable? and, Is it workable? Your answers to these questions help you to select and finalise the topic. In short, you should determine the difficulty level, necessary resources, facilities of guidance, validity and workability of the topic. If your topic does not give satisfactory answers to such questions, it is better to avoid the topic.
3. *Helping agencies*: Once the learner fixes the topic, then you should make a list of agencies to whom you should approach for necessary help during your work on the project. The helping agencies include librarian, science teachers, and resource persons on the concerned topics.
4. *Hypothesis*: You should enable learners to formulate alternative answer to the problem (Hypothesis). For example, the hypothesis for the topic sunlight effects photosynthesis can be stated as 'photosynthesis takes place in the presence of sunlight only'. The hypothesis should be formulated to give a direction to your work.
5. *Try out the Project*: This is the actual stage of working on the project. All the activities mentioned above should be made into action. And

now you can direct your students to work on the selected project on the basis of the hypothesis and available resources.

6. *Project Report*: Reporting is very essential to keep a record of any object of happening. The report should be systematically presented in simple clear language.

   A project report should include the following sections:

   i) Title: The title should be precise and attractive. It should also explore the idea contained in it. For example, sunlight is essential for photosynthesis.
   ii) Abstract: By abstract we mean the essence of the project expressed in a few sentences. It should include almost all the main ideas of the project in about fifty to seventy five words.
   iii) Introduction: This section involves brief description of the topic. This also involves related information, purpose of work, scope and method of investigation and the hypotheses of the study.
   iv) Materials and Methods: In this section, the learners have to write the materials used and the method used for investigation. In the given example, the materials and facilities required are a plotted plant, black paper, dark room, iodine solution, warm water and paper clips. The method used may be experimental method with control.
   v) Observation: Learner should note down your observation from the experiments. All the details of such observation should be given as appendix. In the given example, main observations are 'iodine gives blue colour to starch', 'starch is not produced in the area covered by black paper', etc.
   vi) Conclusion: The major conclusion obtained through the study will be given in this section. Evidences for each conclusion should be given in accordance with each.

       - Application and suggestions: Certain projects have applications and practical suggestions. This should be given clearly, so as to utilise the work fully.
       - Appendix: Detailed information about the observations, graphs, tables, photographs, etc., should be given in the appendix.
       - Bibliography: This is the last section of our project report, which provides a list of books utilised for collecting information with regard to the work.

These are the various components of a science project.

Summing Up

In this Chapter, we have seen that extended curricular activities are very essential as far as science teaching is concerned. The major ideas of the chapter can be summarised as follows

i) Extended curricular activities are extensions of classroom activities.
ii) The important extended curricular activities are science club, science exhibition, science quiz, field trips and science projects.
iii) Science club helps to foster scientific awareness, scientific interest, and ability for scientific investigation.
iv) Science exhibition helps to promote organisation abilities, communication skills and creativity.
v) Science quiz explores new horizons of knowledge.
vi) Field trip provides ample opportunities of real life experience.
vii) Science projects help to satisfy the needs of average and above average students.

CHAPTER 19
Resource Unit

A resource unit should act as the backbone of a teaching unit. The teacher should develop the resource unit for each teaching unit as it is required for the instruction of that chapter. A resource unit helps in the effective instruction of that chapter.

Components of Resource Unit

Resource unit means the all-inclusive materials needed for the instruction of a chapter / a teaching unit, or in short it is the best source of information for chapter/ unit planning. When we get a subject matter, at first we should prepare the resource unit. Perhaps we may not be able to utilise all that is listed in the resource unit at the time of teaching. So from a resource unit, we can make the plan for a chapter, based on the available and utilisable resources.

Now, naturally a question arises: how does a resource unit become all inclusive? We shall get the answer by analysing the components of a resource unit.

1. *List of possible instructional objectives*: The first component of resource unit is a complete list of instructional objectives for the chapter to be taught. A complete list of instructional objectives should be prepared in advance and included in the resource unit.
2. *Subject matter outline*: Next component in resource unit is the subject matter to be included. The subject matter should be selected from authentic sources and should be arranged from ancient to recent information. You should arrange the subject matter outline in separate sections. For example, the subject matter outline for a section of the chapter 'Our environment' can be written as follows.

Chapter : Our Environment

1.1 Concept of ecosystem

  1.1.1 Biotic factors

  1.1.2 Abiotic factors

1.2 Type of ecosystem

1.3 Pond as an ecosystem

  1.3.1 Energy source in a pond

1.3.2 Biotic components in a pond
1.3.3 Abiotic components in a pond

This will continue till the end of the chapter.

3. *Instructional experience*: This is the third component of the resource unit. This includes suggested instructional experience of various types. These instructional experience or activities are designed in such a way as to realise the pupils with different learning abilities are common in our class rooms. So the instructional experience should be different types to cater to the needs of slow learners, fast learners, average learners and differentially abled learners.
4. *Learning aids*: We have discussed the instructional experience as a component of resource unit. Along with that, learning aids are also required for effective instruction. A variety of learning aids should be included in the resource unit for the benefit of learners. These aids can be auditory or visual or audio visual in nature. But maximum possible learning aids should be included in the resource unit.
5. *Bibliography*: A bibliography involves various sources of the content. Appendix and important terminology in the subject outline can also be included.
6. *Sample tests*: This is the final component in a resource unit. This involves sample tests based on the subject matter outline in order to test whether the objectives of the chapter are realised.

These are the components of a resource unit. The materials in the resource unit should be in such a depth that a teacher can build their own teaching unit from this material. It should also be helpful to meet the needs of students with different learning abilities.

Steps in Developing Resource Unit

We have already discussed the components of resource units. In developing a resource unit, the important steps are collection of data, preparation of materials and organisation of materials. We shall discuss each one in detail.

Collection of Data

The first step in developing a resource unit is collection of data. At this step you have to gather information relevant to developing a resource unit. While collecting the relevant data you should take the following points into consideration.

a) ***What should be collected?*** First of all, you should determine what data should be collected? Data related to subject matter, instructional experiences and instructional aids can be collected. Here you should collect these data relevant to the chapter under consideration.

b) ***Sources of information:*** Once you have determine what all things are to be collected, then you should identify the sources from which the data can be collected. The primary source shall be authentic books, research reports, journals and encyclopaedia. In addition to the primary sources, you should collect data from secondary sources also. The secondary sources may include discussion with experts in the field of research. For example, you are going to collect data about nervous system. You should get primary information from books and other publications, and if you need any additional information or classification of any point, you should approach an expert.

Preparation of Materials

In addition to collection of data, you should prepare or develop certain other components of the resource unit also. This includes the following items such as instructional objectives, instructional experiences, learning aids and testing tools.

1. *Instructional objectives*: To achieve mastery in any given content we have to frame certain objectives. For example, for the lesson 'Pollution' we have to frame the objectives such as
   i. *to develop a positive attitude towards pollution control,*
   ii. *to identify the major pollutants, and*
   iii. *to apply ways to control pollution.*

   So you should formulate objectives for the topic you have chosen.
2. *Instructional experience*: The unique contribution of a resource unit is in its variety of instructional experiences. You should include as many number and range of instructional experience in a resource unit, because you have to consider individual differences while you are teaching in mixed ability classes. So instructional experiences catering to the need of average learners and disabled learners are to be there in the resource unit. You should also include varieties of instructional experiences to increase learner's interest and satisfy their needs.
3. *Learning aids*: We know that instructional experiences need the support of learning aids. The type of learning aids required should be determined by the type of instructional experience that you have selected. So, you should develop learning aids that suit all instructional experiences included in the resource unit. You should make a list of learning aids to be included in the chapter.
4. *Testing tools*: Unit test is very familiar to you. In resource unit also, you should include a sample test material. The list should be developed on the basis of the instructional objectives. The list should include different types of test items. Such a model test will be helpful to you to develop suitable questions according to the level of your students.

Organisation of Materials

Organisation of materials mean arrangement of materials in the resource unit in a sequential order. The organisation of materials involves ordering of materials, numbering of items and section wise division of items. Let us discuss each one in detail.

1. *Ordering of materials*: Ordering of materials means arrangement of materials in sequential order. These components are arranged in different groups such as experiences for average learners, learning experiences for below average learners, and learning experiences for above average learners. This will help you to select the appropriate experience as per the needs of the students.
2. *Sectioning and numbering*: Sectioning is dividing the material into suitable sections. Usually, a section consists of details of a single aspect. For example, instructional experience for average learners should be given in one section and that for above average learners should be given in another section.
3. Necessary numbers should be given to components, section and sub sections, if any. It will help to locate a topic very easily.

Illustrative Model of a Resource Unit

Now let us see an illustrative model of a resource unit, we shall discuss the chapter Evolution as example.

Evolution

1. *Instructional Objectives*

The instructional objectives of this resource unit are as follows. The pupils should be able to:

i. Identify scientific terms, scientific facts and concepts relating to evolution.
ii. Interpret the facts and concepts relating to evolution.
iii. Analyse the facts, concepts, principles and theories relating to evolution.
iv. Define the important aspects of evolution.
v. Compare the various aspects of evolution.
vi. Explain scientific basis for evolution.
vii. Generalise concepts, principles and theories of evaluation.
viii. Develop skill in observing various aspects of evolution.
ix. Collect and organise data relating to evolution.
x. Develop interest in the process of evolution.
xi. Develop scientific attitude towards natural phenomena
xii. Develop appreciation of scientific investigation and inventions.

2. *Subject matter outline*

1.1 Definition of organic evolution
  1.1.1 Structural differences of organisms through time
  1.1.2 Time duration as determinant of evolution
1.2 Origin of life
1.3 Theories of origin of life
  1.3.1 Reincarnation theory
    1.3.1.1 Proof in support and against the theory
  1.3.3 Theory of chemical evolution
    1.3.3.1 Proof in support and against the theory
1.4 Condition of the earth at the time of origin of life
1.5 From where did life begin?
1.6 Chemical reaction and evolution
1.7 Important elements related to life
1.8 Nucleo-proteins – first form to life
  1.8.1 Peculiarities of nucleo-proteins
1.9 Unicellular forms of life
  1.9.1 Early unicellular forms
2.0 Multicellular forms of life
  2.0.1 Early multicellular forms
3.0 Evidence of organic evolution
3.1 Paleontological evidences
  3.1.1 Definition of paleontology
  3.1.2 How to determine the age of fossils
  3.1.3 Difference between fossils of different times
  3.1.4 Findings of fossil study
3.2 Comparison of animal body structure
  3.2.1 Similarities in bodily features
  3.2.2 Findings in support of evolution
3.3 Taxonomical evidences of evolution
  3.3.1 How does taxonomy become evidence for evolution
3.4 Embryological evidences
  3.4.1 Features of embryo at different stages of development
  3.4.2 Recapitulation of characters
3.5 Physiological evidences
  3.5.1 Physiology behind various life processes
3.6 Biochemical evidences
  3.6.1 Biochemical similarities of different groups of organisms

4.0 Human evolution

4.1 Ancestors of modern man

4.1.1 Features of various ancestors of human beings

4.2 Advantages of human beings

4.3 Disadvantages of human body

4.4 Conclusion

The variety of instructional experiences possible for this resource unit are as follows.

Questioning is an easy and important experience to explore various aspects of any concept. Questions can be framed according to the classroom situation and progress of the lesson. While teaching evolution, different types of questions can be asked. These should include questions to test the previous knowledge, introductory questions, developmental questions and review questions. Questions to test previous knowledge should give a clear idea about pupils' present knowledge level. Introductory questions help to introduce the new topic in relation with the previous knowledge. Developmental questions are those which are asked during the progress of the lesson. Review questions should be asked at the end of the lesson. Such questions are helpful to know how far the pupils have learned.

Discussion is another instructional experience to a great extent. Important aspects of evolution can be recognised through discussion.

Instructional experiences with the help of specimens, models and diagrams are effective methods.

Observation of natural phenomena such as seed germination, growth of plants and animals, differences between parents and offspring and similarities of parents and offspring is another useful instructional method.

Short films, animations and video clips relating to organic evolution can be effectively utilised for instruction.

Experimentation is another valid method of instruction. For example, students should be encouraged to conduct experiments to disprove self generation theory of evolution.

Field trip is a method which has profound use in the instruction of this unit. Trips to museum, zoo, places of evolutionary importance, tissue culture farms, agriculture farms and animal farms will be helpful to understand varieties and other important processes of evolution.

Learning Aids: Various learning aids which are useful for the instruction are as follows:

i. Pictures and diagrams of ancient earth, plants and animals to show the life at ancient time.
ii. Models and charts of unicellular and multicellular living beings to develop the concept of complexities and bio diversity through time.
iii. Photographs, diagrams and descriptions on fossils to express the nature of paleontology and its significance in evolution.
iv. Specimens and diagrams of developmental stages of different animals to exhibit recapitulation of ancient characteristics during the development of embryos and to show the embryological evidences of evolution.
v. Pictorial view of taxonomy to understand the taxonomical evidence of evolution.
vi. Diagrams of forelimb bones of different animals to show the structural similarities as an evidence of evolution.
vii. Photographs, or diagrams of different human ancestors to develop the concept of human evolution.
viii. Animations and films on fossils and collection of fossils, to understand the available evidence of evolution.

Bibliography

In this section, the various sources from where the subject matter outline and other content of the chapter are obtained are to be given. These should include the author, title of the article, name of Unit or journal, page numbers, publishing company and year of publication. For example, if the material is taken from a book, it should be given as follows

Sharma, S.D. (1990), *Methods of Science Teaching* (First edn), New Delhi, Sterling, pp 120-125.

If the material is from the journal, it should be given as follows:

Suresh, D. (1994), "Human Evolution", in *Journal of Biology,* Vol. 7 (pp. 110-115)

You should also give appendices if present in bibliography. If any terminology requires special reference, it should also be given as glossary.

Sample Test

Sample test items may be written down, if necessary, or the teacher may develop and use test of one's choice. Test should include different types of test items such as objective type, short answer type and essay type items. You should utilise those principles of test construction, which we have discussed already to develop a test of your choice. One sample item for each type of questions is given as follows.

Objective type

1. *The study of fossil is termed as ....*
   Short answer type
2. *What is meant by recapitulation of ancestral characteristics?*
   Essay type
3. *Human body has many limitations, even though human being has become the most powerful species. Explain How?*

(This is the end of an illustration for a resource unit. You should develop and use resource units of your own choice for each unit in science that you have to teach).

Summing Up

We have discussed various aspects of resource unit in this chapter. The major points of our discussion can be summarised as follows:

A. The components of resource unit are
   List of possible instructional objectives
   i) Subject matter outline
   ii) Instructional experiences
   iii) Learning aids
   iv) Bibliography, and
   v) Sample test.

B. The major steps in developing a resource unit are
   i) Collection of data
   ii) Preparation of materials, and
   iii) Organisation of materials.

C. Collection of data involves the ways to collect data, sources of data, and what all things should be collected.

D. Preparation of materials involve developing instructional objectives, instructional experiences.

E. Preparation of materials involves developing instructional objectives, instructional experiences, instructional aids and testing tools.

F. Organisation of materials involves ordering of materials, sectioning and numbering.

UNIT 6

Strategies of Evaluation in Science

Chapter 20

Meaning of Evaluation

Evaluation is the part and parcel of any system of education. We are using a variety of techniques for evaluating outcomes of pupils. The techniques of evaluation are very important and a teacher should adopt sensible and suitable methods for different purposes. Therefore, you should be well in touch with the basic aspects of evaluation. You have to answer three basic questions which help you to understand the concept of evaluation.

Concept of Evaluation

Evaluation, as the name indicates, stands for value judgement. It is the judgement of merit, based on various evidences or findings. These evidences shall be obtained by measuring of various activities and responses of students. Such responses can be oral, written or performance, with respect to the nature of the measurement. So the measurement is the process by which we can measure abilities, and achievement of individuals, but evaluation is something more than measurement, because measurement measures only the quantity of something. If the process is to be turned into evaluation, you should synthesise measurement. Synthesis can be done by converting the scores into certain values, such as the level of achievement, objectives realised, and change in behaviuor or personality, etc. So, measurement is a means by which evaluation is achieved. Evaluation has specific purpose, such as judging which all objectives are achieved; how far it is achieved; and the nature of behavioural changes that have happened in pupils. Now, we shall try to answer the questions such as, why evaluation? what is to be evaluated?, and how to evaluate? Answering these questions will help in understanding the concept of evaluation clearly.

Why Evaluation

Evaluation is directed towards value judgement. Education involves pre-planned formal situations given for the all-round development of pupils. Because it is pre-planned and it will definitely have certain aims and objectives regarding the extent of development of pupils. Therefore, it is judging whether the aims and objectives have been attained and whether the programme is goal directed. It tells us whether the goals of education are attained or not. And if attained, the extent of attainment also may be known. We know that bringing out desirable changes in behaviour of pupil is the primary aim of education. Evaluation has the directive role in making such desirable changes in behaviour.

Suppose, you are teaching science in tenth standard, you may simply develop your class to teach the essential concepts in the given content. You may not attempt to test whether your pupils have learned the ideas or not. You have assumption that your students have learned all the given ideas. But perhaps this will be a wrong assumption as each student has different learning abilities. So it is clear that evaluation is a part of teaching, i.e. evaluation should go hand in hand with instruction then only we will be able to make appropriate behavioural changes in students.

What is to be Evaluated?

Now it is clear that evaluation is essential, so naturally the question arises that what is to be evaluated? Let us try to answer this question.

We have seen that desirable behavioural changes are the target of education. These desirable behavioural changes are otherwise termed as educational objectives or instructional objectives. This term may be a familiar one to you. So, evaluation aims to determine how well educational objectives have been attained. Now, it is essential to know the important instructional objectives. So, let us have a discussion on major instructional objectives.

Instructional Objectives

Since education aims at developing desirable changes in behaviour, each instructional objective stands for developing a particular behaviour. Each instructional objective should be stated in behavioural terms so as to facilitate measurement of the observable behaviour. Planning and designing of instruction is based on objectives. Suitable learning experiences should be used to develop the behaviour up to the desired level. But the problem arises is that we could measure only the observable behaviour. So, we have to state the objectives in observable form. For example, you cannot observe directly whether a student knows all the components of the ecosystem. Here the listing of components will help you to know whether the students know it or not.

Now we will see the major instructional objectives. There are three domains of instructional objectives such as cognitive domain, affective domain and psychomotor domain.

Cognitive domain involves knowledge, intellectual ability and intellectual skills. Affective domain involves attitude, appreciation, social and emotional adjustment, will, character, etc. And the psychomotor domain involves muscular skills and co-ordination. So, you can understand that there are a variety of objectives and specifications under each domain and a variety of evaluation techniques are essential to measure the attainment of all such objectives.

Taxonomy of Objectives

Taxonomy means systematic classification. There are various classifications of objectives, but the classification formulated by Benjamin S. Bloom, et al (1956), and its revision in 2001 by Anderson, et al are the significant ones. Here we will see the classification of objectives under cognitive, affective, and psychomotor domains. Cognitive domain is usually given more emphasis as far as the classroom instruction is concerned.

Table: The Detailed Classification of Cognitive Domain.

Category	*Objectives*	*Action verbs*
A. Knowledge	1. Knowledge of specifics 2. Knowledge of terminology 3. Knowledge of specific facts 4. Knowledge of conventions 5. Knowledge of trends and sequences 6. Knowledge of classification and categories 7. Knowledge of criteriaKnowledge of methodology 8. Knowledge of universals and abstractions 9. Knowledge of principles and generalisation 10. Knowledge of theories and structures	Recall Recognise State List NameGive, Describe
B. Comprehension (Understanding)	1. Translation 2. Interpretation 3. Extrapolation	Translate Illustrate, detect, identify, classify, interpret, compare, select, discriminate explain, calculate, re arrange, manipulate
C. Application	1. Reasoning 2. Definition 3. Suggestion	Make (hypothesis, establish relation, give reasons, reason out, draw inference, prediction, define)

D. Analysis	i) Analysis of elements ii) Analysis of relationships iii) Analysis of organisational principles	Analyse, suggest, find out relation, identify the assumptions, state the theory of principles, predict the effect, specify the limitations
E. Synthesis	a) Production of unique communication b) Production of a plan or proposed set of operations c) Derivation of a set of abstractions	Communicate Organise Derive ProduceFormulate a hypothesis make a generalisation propose an experiment, interpret the data
E. Evaluation	a) Judgement based on internal evidence b) Judgement based on external evidence	Judge, evaluate, defend position, justify, discuss critically, find the fallacy in

In the Table above, the detailed classification of cognitive domain and its categories, objectives and action verbs for each specification are given. The objective under cognitive domain is classified into six categories such as knowledge, comprehension (understanding), application, analysis, synthesis, and evaluation. Each of these objectives should be stated in observable, measurable and attainable forms. Such specific objectives are otherwise termed as specification. Specific objective have two parts such as an action verb and a content part. Action verb is a specific verb used to represent an action in relation to pupils learning behaviour, such as pupil recalls, explains, applies, etc. The content part of the specification will have to change with different content and the action verbs can remain the same.

These six categories were revised in 2001, on the perception that learning outcomes are better measured in terms of process. Hence, the categories were revised as Remembering, Understanding, Applying, Analysing, Evaluating and Creating; instead of Knowledge, Understanding, Application, Synthesis and Evaluation.

Another significant taxonomy, especially for science education, is the one which is framed by McCormack and Yager in 1989. According to this classification the five domains are, Knowledge (Knowing and

Understanding), Process (Exploring and Discovering), Creativity (Imagining and Creating) Application (Using and Applying), Attitude (Feeling and Valuing)

Statement of objectives in observable and measurable form alone gives direction in evaluation. An example for correct statement of an objective in behavioural terms is given below.

Statement of Objective

General Statement: Knows a synonym for animal (such as living being, creature) – *Statement in behavioural term*

Writes (or states or selects) a synonym, for the term animal.

You should formulate objectives in behavioural terms using each action verb and the related content part.

How to Evaluate

Now, we shall discuss various procedures of evaluation which helps to measure attainment of educational objectives and personality changes in your students. The following are various evaluation techniques and tools to measure behavioural changes in students.

The important techniques of evaluation can be classified as follows.

a) Achievement testing
b) Self reporting techniques
c) Observational techniques
d) Miscellaneous techniques
e) Case study techniques
f) Diagnostic testing

There are specific tools for evaluation under each technique. The tools under each technique are given below.

Tools for Evaluation

Achievement testing	*Achievement test*
Self reporting techniques	Inventory, questionnaire, opinionaire and check list.
Observational techniques	Observational check list, rating scale, situational test and anecdotal records
Miscellaneous techniques	Analysis of records and documents interview, sociometry, Guess Who technique and social distance scale
Case study technique	All tools
Diagnostic testing	Diagnostic test

Tests can be classified on the basis of content, format, mode of construction and mode of administration.

Among the tests listed above, the tests measuring achievement is the familiar test. Achievement test is most important as far as classroom teaching is concerned, because you have to use achievement tests frequently. Other techniques such as sociometric techniques, observation interview, anecdotal records, etc., are also useful in evaluating pupil behaviour.

Techniques of sociological nature will help you to determine the socio-emotional development, acceptance, leadership qualities, adjustment problems, etc. of your students. You shall get the detailed discussion of such techniques.

Types of Tests

Tests are tools, specified for measuring something through the process of testing and this measurement helps us in evaluation. Different types of tests serve for checking the realisation of various purposes of education. These tests may be categorised into three, such as:

- Purpose Specific Tests
- Mode Specific Tests
- Process Specific Tests

Though we have categorised the tests into three, there can be inter relations between them and we could not separate them into water tight compartments.

Purpose Specific Tests

This category involves those tests which are designed to achieve specific purposes. The major tests coming under this category are:Diagnostic tests,Aptitude tests,Achievement tests, andProficiency tests.

Diagnostic tests – The diagnostic tests help us to identify the points where the learners need remedial coaching. These will help us to know actually what students know, and what they do not know. In order to serve these purposes, diagnostic tests should be prepared by covering all details of the given content.

Aptitude test – These types of tests help to identify special abilities in particular areas. These abilities should be indicative of future performance. Aptitude for different profession, musical aptitude, aptitude for teaching, etc. can be measured separately. These tests are generally used to select people for courses requiring special abilities.

Achievement test – You may be familiar with the purpose of achievement tests. They are used to measure the extent to which the instructional objectives have been realised. These tests are usually designed on the basis of the prescribed syllabus for each subject and standard.

Proficiency test – Proficiency tests are usually used to assess the general ability of a person at a given time. Practical test for proficiency in typewriting is an example for proficiency test.

Mode Specific Tests

In mode-specific category of tests we can include five pairs of test types. Tests in each pair are different from another on the basis of the nature of the test. The main categories are as follows.

a) Formal assessment vs. Informal assessment
b) Formative assessment vs. Summative assessment
c) Course work vs. Examination
d) Process vs. Product assessment
e) Internal assessment vs. External assessment

Formal assessment vs. Informal assessment: Formal assessment is used for selection on the basis of any special achievement for scholarships or awards. This should follow a standardised pattern. The assessment result should be open to public. Merit scholarship is an example for formal assessment.

Informal assessment may be conducted informally to understand the present nature of a given issue. A series of questions to know the pollutants in a locality is an example for informal assessment.

Formative assessment vs. Summative assessment: Formative assessment is assessing the progress in attainment at regular intervals. Formative assessment helps to identify learner's weakness and help learning more easily. Unit tests are example for formative assessment.

Summative assessment or terminal assessment is done at the end of a course, which aims at certifying or grading the attainment. Example: CBSE or SSLC examination.

Course work vs. Examination: Both of these serve the purpose of summative evaluation. Course work may be taken as an index for learner assessment in some cases. Practice teaching during B.Ed. course is an example for course work and its evaluation is the assessment on the basis of the course work.

Examination is a very familiar form of assessment. You are conducting examinations after completing each chapter as unit test, example: unit tests.

Process vs. Product assessment: These types of evaluation are done in experimental and research work. You can assess the performance at different stages leading to the completion of the work or course. This is process assessment. If you make assessment on the basis of the final result then it is product assessment.

Internal assessment vs. External assessment: Internal assessment is a type of assessment in which the teacher assesses certain components as a part of continuous progress of learners. Achievement in both academic and non-academic areas may be considered for internal assessment. In external assessment, the evaluator is an outsider, that is, from other institution or other state.

Process- Specific Tests

Process-specific tests can be categorised on the basis of its construction. The major types of tests coming under this category are.

A. Teacher made test vs. Standardised test, and
B. Norm referenced test vs. Criterion referenced test

Teacher-made test vs. Standardised test: A teacher made test is the one which is constructed by a teacher for the use in his /her own classroom. Teacher is the ultimate authority who determines the scope of the test, type of test items, number of items and scoring procedure.

Standardised tests are produced on a large scale by a group of experts in a subject by establishing its objectivity and accuracy. They are developed using strict rules. The scoring and interpretation also will have to follow specific instructions.

Norm referenced test vs Criterion referenced test: A norm referenced test helps us to identify the level of achievement of each student or the ability of each student assessed in comparison with a standard norm (specific level of attainment) Example: Medical entrance test.

A criterion referenced test helps to assess the ability of a student against a select criterion. A criterion here includes a set of performance, based on the standard developmental changes expected. This test helps to specify the ability of a student in behavioural terms. Example: Practical test in typewriting.

These are the different types of tests used for evaluating various abilities of your students.

We shall have a discussion on classroom testing and constructing an achievement test in Chapter 2 of this unit. Now, we shall discuss certain new ideas such as minimum levels of learning and internal assessment.

Minimum Levels of Learning

As teachers, we know the term 'learning' very well. Now we shall discuss about levels of learning. Level of learning means the depth of learning of a subject. In the learning of every subject, it is essential to learn the basic aspects of the subject. For example, in order to learn a new language, first of all learning the alphabets of that language is essential. Likewise, study of mathematics requires the knowledge of basic mathematical operations such as, addition, deletion, multiplication and division. The basic aspects or essential aspects of every subject act as the foundation for learning that subject in depth. If one does not learn the basic aspects of a subject, s/he will not be able to study the subject in depth.

The learning of these basic aspects or essential aspects of a subject is referred to as minimum level of learning of that subject. The minimum level of learning required to study a subject will have to change according to the changes in depth of learning. So the minimum level of learning science at secondary level is entirely different from that of the primary level and that at the higher secondary level.

As teachers you must know the minimum level of learning science at secondary level. They are: the knowledge of living beings, characteristics of living beings, important life processes, and economic aspects of living beings. You should test your students to know whether they have attained the minimum level of learning. If your students did not learn these aspects, you should help them to learn the essential basic aspects.

Internal Assessment

Internal assessment is a specific form of evaluation. We need to make two types of measurement, namely quantitative and qualitative measurement. Quantitative measurement is usually done by examinations. But qualitative measurement can be obtained by internal assessment. Internal assessment means assessment of learners continuously by the teacher by using various measures. Both academic and non-academic achievement should be considered for internal assessment. Thus, internal assessment helps us to give a comprehensive picture of the student's progress in achievement. Internal assessment also helps us to evaluate the attainment of the long range objectives. Now, let us see the different modes of internal assessment.

Modes of Internal Assessment

We can identify different modes of internal assessment. The first mode of internal assessment is through tests, and tests are of various types. You should conduct periodical, oral and written tests for the purpose of internal assessment. The written tests used for this purpose are unit tests and term end tests. Oral tests are those which we conduct at any time in the classroom or at laboratory.

Laboratory work is the second mode of internal assessment. Practical work and various lab works conducted by the students should be used to measure his ability in laboratory work. And this ability is considered for internal assessment.

Assignments are another mode of internal assessment. Assignments should be given at periodical intervals in connection with each unit. An assignment question can be as follows:

"Critically analyse the causes of pollution and lethal effects of pollution on environment."

Participation in sports and games can be considered for internal assessment, if you are aiming at comprehensive development of children. Weightage should be given for participation at higher levels (district or state level). Assessing participation in co-curricular activities also is a mode of internal assessment. Here also you should give appropriate weightage for performance at district and state levels. The co-curricular activities may include debates, elocution, drawing, music, drama, writing for school magazines and participation in exhibition.

These are the areas that can be utilised for internal assessment. Though internal assessment helps to measure qualities of learners, it has also some disadvantages.

It may result in subjectivity from the part of teachers. Some teachers may misuse this in some cases. Thus, internal assessment should be used judiciously.

Summing Up

In this chapter we have discussed the concept of evaluation, the rationale for evaluation, the focus of evaluation, different tests for evaluation, minimum levels of learning and internal assessment.

Evaluation helps to judge the achievement of objectives and thereby behavioural changes.

The focus of evaluation should be instructional objectives, which are stated in observable and measurable form.

Various techniques such as achievement testing, self reporting techniques observational techniques, miscellaneous techniques, case study and diagnostic testing are used for evaluation.

Minimum levels of learning mean the basic and essential aspects of every subject which could be learnt in lower classes and is necessary for further learning.

Written tests, laboratory work, assignments, participation in curricular and co-curricular activities, etc., should be taken for internal assessment.

Chapter 21
Test Construction

Introduction

In our daily life, we have to face a number of tests of different types. Testing is usually done for assessing particular changes in behaviour. If you want to administer a test, the testing techniques should be familiar to you. A poorly constructed test does not serve the purpose of the test.

Phases of Testing

Educational evaluation is closely related to teaching. You (teacher) should use a variety of testing techniques to evaluate student's performance. Usually, you should develop various tests to assess the performance of test development. There are different phases in development of tests. Before we discuss these phases in detail, you may do the following learning activity.

Deciding topic, writing test items, fix number of test item, and scoring key for tests. We have to discuss each of these steps and some other steps as phase of testing. Mainly there are five phases for classroom testing. They are planning, design, development; administration of the test, and communication of result. Let us discuss each one in detail.

Planning for Testing

This is the first phase of classroom testing, and planning is the first phase of every activity.

How to plan for the test?: You may have opined that the date, duration, and time of the test should be planned in advance. Exactly, you must do these. But along with these aspects, you should consider the following components as the main concern at planning phase. The main components are instructional goals and objectives, expected level of learning outcomes, and provision of remedial work. Let us see each of these components in detail.

Instructional goals will be a familiar aspect for all of you. Instruction usually aims to attain specific goals or objectives. You should have written instructional objectives for each lesson that you have to teach. So you should first of all identify the instructional objectives of the chapter/ unit.

You will have some expectations about your student's performance. You may have expected a particular level of achievement from each individual and the group as whole. For example, you are teaching at tenth standard. So naturally, you may expect that the front benchers will be high achievers than back benchers. This kind of assumption about achievement is referred to as expected level of learning outcomes.

Another thing we should consider while planning is the provision remedial of work. Though remedial work comes after interpretation of test result, you should be ready for it early enough.

Design of the Test

The second phase of testing is design of test.

Design means structural specification of the test. Structural specification includes type of test, type of test items, objectives of the chapter/unit, difficulty level of test items, scoring key and marking scheme. All these aspects together are termed as blueprint of the test. What you should do at this phase is to make the blue print of the test. In doing so, you should select different types of test items namely multiple choice type, short answer type and essay type. You should fix the number of items in each type of items. And these items should be based on objectives of the chapter/unit.

Developing a Test

The third phase of testing is developing a test.

Now you are ready to develop a test of your choice, as you have prepared the blue print. The writing of test items is done at this phase.

You might have remembered that length of the item, structure of the item, clarity and the familiarity are essential points to be taken into consideration, while writing test items.

Too lengthy test item will confuse your students, so you may not get the correct response meant for it. Therefore, the items should be short and precise, such as:

"Give the name of two desert animals."

The items should be grammatically correct and should involve a single aspect. *Example*

"Write the essential features of flowers, leaves, fruits, roots, and plants."

You should not ask questions like this. Instead, you should split this question into five questions, each of them carrying a single aspect, such as flower, leaf, fruit, root and plant.

Clarity of the test item is very important. If the item is not clear the students will not understand what is expected and you will not get a desired response. So you should write the items in simple, clear and straight forward language and you must use familiar words to write test items.

Along with these points you should consider the following points also, while writing the test items.

a) The items must be based on the content of the chapter/unit.
b) The content and situations given in items should be familiar to learners.
c) Appropriate instructions should be given where ever necessary. For example, *"Questions 1 to 8 carry one mark each. Write a word or sentence as the answer."*
   Now let us discuss

Administration of the Test

The fourth phase of testing is administration of the test.

Test Administration is familiar process for you. Let us see what you will do for test administration.

You may have remarked that while administering the test, the main concern is on facilities in the classroom.

Classroom facilities, such as, enough lighting, and ventilation are very essential to conduct a learner-friendly test. Enough space should be provided to facilitate convenient seating of students. The time fixed for administering the test should not involve intervals of the class. If intervals come in between the test, the noise and distractions from outside and other classes will adversely affect the answering process.

Communication of Test Result

The fifth phase of testing is communication of test results.Pupils are very eager to know their test score and grades. So it is very essential to communicate the grades properly and timely. It is also essential to communicate their progress at the end of each term. Communication of results helps your students to make necessary changes in their study habits. For example, a student who is able to achieve higher grades, could not achieve the expected level of the first unit test. Then ask them about their study habits, duration and time of study. This will help you to give necessary guidelines to the students in order to improve their achievement. The knowledge of progress will also motivate pupils for further learning.

Types of Test Items

An item means a question. In response to an item the learner has to express what s/he is supposed to have acquired during instruction. Usually a question or an item is based on a specification of an educational objective, which demands a response from the learner. Such responses are subject to evaluation. Usually items are arranged in item formats. An item format means the format or the style of a question, for example, a multiple choice item, completion type item, etc. Item formats are classified mainly into two categories namely selection type and supply type item formats.

Selection Type Item Formats

In selection type item format, answers are provided along with the items. The answers are given in a cluster of similar type of incorrect answers. Learners have to choose the correct answer from the group of answers. Since there will be only one correct answer for these items, the scoring can be done objectively. Therefore, they are known as objective type also. Three types of item can be included in this.

Multiple Choice items: Multiple choice items are essential part of any achievement test. You may be familiar with this type of items. In this type, the learner has to choose the correct answer from the given options, normally four in number. These types of items should be either in the form of an incomplete statement or as an interrogative question. *Example.*

Item No. 1.

Animals live in water are called..................

a) Fishes
b) Water beings
c) Aquatic animals
d) Terrestrial animals

Item No. 2.

Which one is a renewable natural resource?

i. Iron
ii. Rubber
iii. Petroleum
iv. Aluminium

Item 1 is an example for an incomplete statement form and item 2 is an example for interrogative question form.

True or False items: Here, learner is to select the correct answer from the two given alternatives. True or false items are usually represented as statements. Learner can make his/her response by putting a tick mark at the relevant place.

Matching type items: Matching type items can be used when the content has a number of related concepts, e.g. scientists and their inventions; books and authors; animals and their habitats.

Supply Type Item Formats

Supply type item requires supply of responses in relation to the questions. In certain item types only one word is required as answer, but in some other item types very long responses are necessary. In this category of item format also, there are three types of items. They are completion type items, short answer type items and essay type items.

Completion type items: In completion type items, the learner is to supply one word or two words to make the statement complete and meaningful. The format of this type comprises of an incomplete statement. You should take care to make the item clear by completing the statement. See the following example, *Animals living on ....*

Here the learner cannot give correct answer, because the statement is a bit confusing. So you should restate the item so as to direct the learners to know what actually we expect from them.

You should always take care of while preparing such items. These completion type items are also scored objectively.

Short Answer type items: Short answer type items are also the essential component of an achievement test. Short answer type items are useful to measure abilities such as analysis, synthesis and evaluation. Learner should be thorough with the use of language and diagrams in order to answer such questions. Here also, you should state the question clearly so that the scope should be clear. See the following example.

Write short note on pollution. This type of question statement is defective so let us try to modify the item as follows: *Write in about fifty words the lethal effects of pollution on environment*: If the question is not clearly stated, the learner may not answer correctly or up to the required depth of the content.

Essay type items: Essay type items also may be familiar to you. Essay type items help us to measure.

1. Learner's ability to use language.
2. Learner's ability in organisation and presentation of data precisely and accurately.
3. It also helps to measure abilities such as application, analysis, synthesis and evaluation. You should take care to state the question clearly and to give necessary directions such as length of the answer. See the following example.

Write an essay in not more than 200 words about air pollution; its causes, lethal effects and preventive measures.

There are different item formats which can be utilised for test construction. Now we shall pass into planning for testing.

Planning for Testing

Specify Course Content and Objectives

Once you plan to evaluate your students, then you should specify the actual content area on which the test should be developed. Now, naturally a question will arise as to what is to be evaluated. You have to evaluate the achievement of pupils. We have defined achievement in terms of attaining instructional objectives. So, you should evaluate whether those objectives have been realised or not. For example, you decide to conduct the test on the chapter 'Our Environment'. You should test the realisation of objectives such as *draw inferences, establish relationships, interpret cause-effect relationship, sketch and label diagrams* and so on. In order to test the realisation of these objectives, you have to select appropriate item formats.

Selection of Appropriate Item Format

Several item formats are available to use in a variety of situations. The selection of item formats depends on:

i) the content area,
ii) purpose of the test, and
iii) duration of the test.

You have to select necessary number and types of item formats as per your need. You should involve necessary number of objective type, short answer type and essay type of items.

Preparing Test Question Paper

We have already discussed different types of item formats and planning for testing. Now let us see the aspects in construction of a test question paper.

Instructional Objectives

You have to list out the instructional objectives, as the first step in the construction of a question paper. This listing will help you to determine the required number of items under the format along with the objectives and specification. They are given as follows. K-Knowledge, U-Understanding, A-Application, S-Skill, K-Recalls, K (Recognises), U (Discriminates, compares, classifies, detect, cites illustrations, verifies, generalises, etc.), A (Analyses, formulate hypothesis, judges, give reasons, etc.), S (Measures, reads, records, sketches, drawings, etc.). Once you had enlisted the objectives, then you should develop a blue print.

Blue Print

Blue print is a three dimensional chart showing the type of items, objectives and number of items in each category. The major steps in designing a blue print. involve assigning weightages to content, objectives, difficulty level, and type of items. Scheme of options and scheme of sections also should be decided. Now let us see the details of each step for developing a blue print for a unit test on the chapter cell.

Formation of Questions

Questions of your choice can be prepared on the basis of the blue print. The questions should be arranged in different sections. You have to formulate the items as we have discussed in section on types of test items.

Scoring Key

A scoring key should be prepared after preparing the question. This will act as a guideline for scoring the responses of learners. The scoring key should include question numbers, value points and score. In the case of objective type questions, letters representing correct answers should be given along with the question numbers.

Summing Up

In this chapter we have discussed phases of testing, types of test items, planning for testing and preparing a test question paper. The process of testing involves the following phases.

1. Planning for testing
2. Design of the test
3. Developing a test
4. Administering the test
5. Communication of the test result

The major types of test items are:

- i) Selection type – multiple choice, true or false and matching type
- ii) Supply type – completion type, short essay and essay

Planning for testing involves what is to be listed. Specify course content and objectives, and selection of appropriate item formats.

Preparation of test question paper involves fixing of instructional objectives, blue print, formulation of questions and scoring key.

Chapter 22

Self Reporting Techniques

Usual type of test may not serve all purposes of the evaluator. So you have to know some other evaluating techniques apart from the regular classroom tests. The usual test will give us the information of achievement only. As a teacher, we should know the needs and opinions of your students. Usually students are hesitant to express their feelings directly to their teacher. Here, details of self reporting techniques such as inventory, questionnaire, opinionnaire and checklist are discussed.

Concept

It is, as the name indicates, a technique used for evaluation in which the students themselves are reporting their own details. The self expression of the learners would be utilised through these techniques. This would help us to understand the personnel opinions of learners in many respects.

The major types of self reporting techniques are inventories, questionnaires, opinionnaires, and check lists.

Inventories

The meaning of inventories and how to develop them are discussed as follows.

Meaning

Inventories lead us to reveal self of students with regard to their various aspects. An inventory attempts to measure a typical behaviour. For example, musical interest inventory attempts to measure the learners' interest in music. Inventories can be developed and used on any particular topic. Generally interest inventories are used widely to understand the preferences of learned in a particular area.

When we want to collect the respondent's family data, personal data, educational plans, we could use inventories. Learner's interest, attitude and personality are also measured using inventories. Now, let us see how to develop an inventory.

Developing an Inventory

The following points should be born in mind, while developing an inventory:

- Define the general and specific objectives
- Construction of appropriate questions or statements
- Arrangement of questions in appropriate order
- Design appropriate format
- Administration of inventory

General and Specific Objectives

The definition of objectives helps us to formulate appropriate questions on the basis of the objectives.

Arrangement of Questions: The questions or statements should be arranged in appropriate groups. This will help tabulation and interpretation of responses. You should arrange the questions in different sections or groups. For example, in a status inventory of pupils we may have sections such as personal data. So you have to arrange questions or statements about one aspect in the same section.

Design of format: The format of the inventory should be attractive, well organised and legibly printed. Care should be taken to leave enough space between the lines. An attractive format will always inspire the learners in answering with full interest.

Administration procedure: Administer the inventory at the appropriate time and place. Ensure a good climate while administering it. You have to state the purpose of the inventory and directions to respond to it, preferably in printed form along with the inventory as an introduction.

Questionnaire

Questionnaire is used to collect factual information. They are otherwise termed as inquiry forms, as they attempt to inquire about various aspects at the given time. Questionnaire should provide us the data of existing status of the conditions we are searching for.

Form of a Questionnaire

A questionnaire may have two forms, namely the closed form and an open form.

Closed form: Questionnaire that demands restricted responses is called closed form. For example, an item require the responses either YES / No is a closed form.

Open form: The open form is just contrary to the closed form. In this type, the respondents are free to express their responses. There is no restriction such as Yes/ No.

Developing a Questionnaire

We can identify the following steps in developing a questionnaire:

- Collection of background knowledge
- Defining the purpose
- Designing of questionnaire
- Finalisation of questionnaire

Collection of background knowledge: You have to collect the background information about the area in which you are going to develop the questionnaire. You will get necessary information through reading books and articles relevant to the area, and also studying other questionnaires. So you will get an overall view of questionnaire, its organisation, and content. You can also consult experts in the relevant fields to gather information regarding the questionnaire.

Defining the purpose: Purpose definition is the next step in developing questionnaires. We can develop questionnaire for different purposes. For example, we should develop a questionnaire on the causes of educational backgrounds of SC and ST students. We can also develop a questionnaire for different sections of people namely for teachers, parents, students, social workers, etc. Whatever level we choose, the purpose should be specified first.

Designing of questionnaire: Questionnaire should be designed either in closed form or open form or in union of closed and open forms. A questionnaire comprising of both closed form and open form is preferable. The questions should be arranged section-wise. Related questions should be given under the same section. The items should be simple, clear and precise. Now let us see the finalisation of questionnaire.

Finalisation of questionnaire: After preparing the questionnaire, you should critically analyse each item. This would help to make any corrections, if necessary. For this purpose, you should write each item on separate item cards. So it helps us to replace the cards or change the order and sequence of questions. After finalising the sequence of items, the questionnaire should be subjected to a pilot test.

For this purpose, it should be given to a very limited number of the students. Through this test we can understand the pitfalls of the questionnaire and the time required to fill it up. By removing the pitfalls, we can finalise the questionnaire.

Opinionnaire

Opinionnaire is a form of questionnaire, through which we can collect opinions about various tasks.

Meaning

Opinionnaire is information form that attempts to measure beliefs of an individual. Researchers must depend upon what people say about their beliefs and feelings. Thus, we could collect and measure opinions.

Opinions are what people really believe. These opinions can be measured using opinionnaire consisting of a number of statements. The respondents are required to mark in itself their degree of agreement or disagreement with the statements as we have seen in inventories.

Developing an Opinionnaire

We can identify the following steps in developing an Opinionnaire:

i) Collection of statements.
ii) Trial test.
iii) Finalisation of Opinionnaire.

Developing an opinionnaire shares many similarities with that of the questionnaire. We must identify the purpose of the opinionnaire before we go for it. First step in developing an opinionnaire is collection of statements.

Collection of statements: A number of statements should be collected at this stage. These should be obtained by background reading of relevant books and articles and discussion with experts. Each statement should be written as in the questionnaire items. This would be written on item card as in the case of questionnaire items. This would help to correct the statements, if required.

Trial test: After arranging the statements, it should be administered to a limited number of students; this pilot testing will help to eliminate confusing and defective statements. We should also be able to understand the time required to complete the tool.

Finalisation of questionnaire: After the trial test, we could eliminate unnecessary items. The number of responses should be fixed as 3 to 5. The responses should be *agree/ undecided / disagree (3 point) or strongly agree/ agree/ undecided/ disagree/ strongly disagree (5 points)*

The scale values for the points are as follows

		Favouring Scale Value	Opposing Scale value
a	Strongly agree	5	1
b	Agree	4	2
c	Undecided	3	3
d	Disagree	2	4
e	Strongly disagree	1	5

We can analyse the scale value of each statement and understand the opinion of the pupil.

Check List

Meaning

A check list means a list of behaviours or activities to which the respondent should mark their responses by putting a tick mark against those which exists. You might have seen check lists in connection with many application forms. See the illustration. At the end of the application form a check list is given.

- *Proof of age*
- *Copies of educational qualifications*
- *Passport size photograph*
- *Income certificate*

Here the check list helps you to check whether all the items have been enclosed with the application. But in check list for self reporting data collection purpose, one has to report oneself against the behaviours or activities which are listed in the check list. Now let us see how to develop a check list.

Developing a Checklist

In the development of a checklist also we have to collect necessary statements at first as per our purpose. The statements should be arranged in logical order. You should administer it to a small group to identify the shortcomings and confusing items. Then you should finalise the checklist after necessary corrections. Use short, simple and clear statements.

Summing Up

In this chapter we have discussed various self reporting techniques such as inventories, questionnaire, opinionnaire and check list.

1. Inventory aims to measure preference or the extent of any behaviour of an individual.
2. Questionnaire should give us data on the existing status of the condition we are searching for. It may have two forms — closed form and open form.
3. Opinionnaire is an information form, which is used to measure belief of an individual.
4. Self reporting checklist is used to collect necessary details of one's behaviour, by making a tick mark to the appropriate degree.

Chapter 23
Observational Techniques

Observation is a natural and common method to get the sociological aspects of an incident or situation. There are specified observational techniques to make our observation precise and correct. What we should do is to become familiar with those observational techniques which help you to assess your pupils.

Observational Checklist

Observational checklist consists of students (name/ number), their activities and behaviours which the observer should record when an incident occurs. But in self reporting checklist, one should report about oneself. This checklist helps us to understand the important characteristics of learners. But we could not rate the quality and frequency of occurrence of behaviour. The observational checklist helps to identify the specified behaviour of learners.

Developing Observational Checklist

We can identify the following steps in developing a checklist.

- Identification of purpose
- Collection of statement
- Arrangement of statement trial testing
- Finalisation of the checklists

Identification of purpose: First of all you should identify the purpose of the checklist, i.e. what characteristics should be observed and recorded. For instance, in order to study the habits of pupils you should collect statements related to study habits and arrange them properly.

Collection of statements: Once we have defined the purpose of the checklist, necessary statements regarding the topic should be collected. These could be collected from the related literature and discussion with experts. You can break up the proposed behaviour so small that it also enables you to develop statements.

Arrangement of statements: The statements should be arranged in logical order. The related statements should be arranged in association with one another. The section-wise grouping will help you to record observation easily.

Trial testing: A pilot administration of the checklist to a limited number of students can be done. This will help us to check the appropriateness of the statements and also its ordering.

Finalisation of the checklist: After the pilot testing, you should make necessary changes in the checklist. Ordering should be finalised and proper directions can be given in introduction.

Rating Scales

Rating scale has many similar characteristics with checklists. But rating scale has some advantages over checklist. Through checklists we can identify whether a characteristic is present or not. But rating scale help us to find out the quality of the behaviour also. The rater (one who records the observations of a rating scale) should have a crucial role in rating scales. Therefore, different types of rating scales are used.

Types of Rating Scales

The major types of rating scales are:

a) Numerical rating scale.
b) Graphic rating scale.
c) Descriptive graphic rating scale.

Numerical rating scale: This is the simplest type of rating scale. In this type, the given characteristics area numbered from 1 to 5. Each number represents the degree of the given characteristics. Usually necessary directions to the rater are given at the beginning along with the key for each digit.

Graphic rating scale: In this type of rating scales, the ratings are made in a graphic form. Here you should assign some value to a specific characteristic. A number of characteristics should be used in serial order. This enables you to construct a behavioural profile of your student.

Descriptive graphic rating scale: This type of rating scale is a detailed version of graphic rating scale that will help to clarify and define behaviour in detail.

This will help us to increase objectivity of rating.

Anecdotal Records

This is another type of device which helps us to record the behaviour of our students. The behaviour should be on specific incidents and situations but in informal settings. For example, a student in the library, laboratory, play ground, group work could be assessed informally using this tool.

Features of Anecdotal Records

Let us see an example to see the features of anecdotal record.

July 10, 1995, 9.30 am

A. Dasheen is seen at the science corner, reading articles on nature, though the regular school work has not begun.

July 25, 1995, 11.30 am (Biology period)

B. Dasheen is found to be the only boy responding to the teachers' questions of certain recent aspects on destruction of nature.

July 28, 1995, 12.15 am (Language period)

C. Dasheen was caught reading a book on nature during the language period and was sent out from the class room.

Interpretation: Dasheen is very interested in natural science

Recommendation: Dasheen should be encouraged to do certain projects related to nature and also to give more attention to other subjects.

We shall try to analyse the hidden features of anecdotal record from this example.

1. It gives the description of an event with regard to its data and time, what had happened and the situation in which it happened.
2. The records are of a series of incidents round about particular aspects.
3. Each anecdotal record should contain a record of a single student.
4. The incident recorded should have significance in the growth and development of the pupil.
5. Interpretation and recommendation should be given separately at the end of the description.

From this we could see that anecdotal records will give us a picture of the specific behaviours of a single student.

Effective Use of Anecdotal Records

While using the anecdotal records you should take care of the following points.

a) Observe only one or two behaviours at a time.
b) Observation should be selective.
c) A guideline for observation should be prepared in advance.
d) Try to collect complete details of the incident.
e) Record should be collected by all the teachers.
f) Enough practice and training should be given to the teachers in observation and writing the anecdotal records.

Situational Test

Situational test is a form of observational techniques which help to assess the students at specific situations.

Meaning of Situational Test

You may create many artificial situations while teaching. For example, in order to introduce respiration, an incident of a child falling in water can be a suitable situation.

You might be of the opinion that a situation can be a special set up including some of the necessary elements for the learning of a given idea. Along with a situation, perception of pupils towards the ideas is also necessary. For example, *you are going to teach breathing, you may narrate about a boy, who does not know swimming. You would then ask a question, what will happen if the boy falls in water? And what is the reason for that? Here you should explore the concept — air is necessary for breathing.*

Thus, you can introduce respiration very well. Such situations are very essential for meaningful learning. Here we shall see a different use of situation, i.e. its use in testing.

Create a situation to measure the response of your students in that situation. Here the students are unaware that they are going to be tested, and only the teacher knows the purpose of that situation. So, situational test is the creation of an artificial situation, in order to test certain specific behaviour in specific situations. The extent of honesty, cooperation, leadership, etc. can be tested of children through this method.

How to Conduct Situational Tests

Development of a suitable situation is the first step in conducting situational tests. It is your duty to select or develop such suitable situations. After selecting the situation, you should expose your children to that situation without their knowledge. You should then observe the behaviour of your students in the situation. It is better to observe them secretly. For example, you are creating a situation to test the honesty of selected pupils in your class. You may create the following situation to test this. You put your purse full of money (you alone know the actual amount) in a corner of your class, when all the pupils are out of the class for interval. It will appear as it was accidently fallen down. You can assign certain outdoor duties to all of the pupils, except for those who are selected to be exposed to the situation. You should allow the pupils (those who have no duties) to go into the classroom. Here you may get three types of response from your pupils. They may be, as follows:

i) The pupils suddenly bring your purse to you or to any responsible person.
ii) The pupils took your purse for them.
iii) The pupils take some money from the purse and put it at the same place.

From these responses you can understand the extent of honesty of your pupils. Likewise you can create situations to test the leadership qualities, co-operation, etc. of your pupils. You can also create situations to test creativity and memory power of your pupils.

Summimg Up

We have discussed various observational techniques, such as observational checklist, rating scale, anecdotal records, and situational tests.

a) Observational checklist is different from that of self reporting checklist in the sense that an outside observer marks the characteristics of pupils in the checklist, instead of reporting by self.
b) Rating scales help to identify the characteristics present in an individual along with its quantity. There are numerical, graphic and descriptive graphic rating scales.
c) Anecdotal records are used to collect specific behaviour of students in informal settings.
d) Situational test proceeds through development of an artificial situation, student's exposure to such situations and observation without the knowledge of students. This test is used to study specific behavioural at specific situations.

Chapter 24

Miscellaneous Techniques

We have already discussed a wide variety of evaluation techniques, which help you to assess your pupils in different ways. We have to consider these miscellaneous techniques and tools which will help to assess various aspects of students also. Miscellaneous techniques such as analysis of records and documents, interview, sociometry, guess who techniques and social distance scale are discussed here.

Analysis of Records and Documents

All of us are familiar with various types of records and documents in our educational institutions. Many of those are very much valuable as far as education of the students is concerned. Now let us make an overview of records and documents used to keep the details of pupils in our school.

Types of Records and Documents

You might have the opinion that items such as admission register, attendance register, health report, sports and games register, art festival register, and awards and scholarship register are necessary documents.

Apart from these, the cumulative record is another very important record containing information of pupil.

All other documents except cumulative record are familiar to us because we are responsible for maintaining all those documents. So you can directly gather information from those records as and when necessary. Now we shall have a discussion on cumulative record — what is it?

Cumulative Record: A cumulative record is a valuable record of information about students. The term cumulative stands for adding information for updating. We could record various types of information in this form. They are:

i) Academic achievement
ii) Class attendance
iii) Assignment responses
iv) Intelligence
v) Health report
vi) Hobbies
vii) Likes and dislikes
viii) Extracurricular activities
ix) Performance for activities

Information about these aspects will help us to understand a child completely. We can verify this as part, say habit on achievement of any of the mentioned aspects and compare it with their recent performance in that aspect can be done.

Interview

Interview is considered as an oral questionnaire in some instances. In questionnaire the respondent is responsible to mark or write the responses. But interview is a face to face situation to gather relevant information from the interviewee. Interview is said to be a powerful tool to gather relevant information, at times, when we may need it in depth. Interview is very useful when we deal with school children.

Types of Interview

Structured Interview: Structured or formal interview means interviewing with a written schedule. Here schedule means all the questions to be asked at the interview. Such a written schedule or format will guide the interviewer to conduct the interview. Since all the questions are predetermined, we can call it as structured or formal.

The questions in the schedule can be of two types, namely, an open format and a closed format. An open form question or open ended question means a question that requires response in depth. For example, you want to know the response of your students about the use of pesticides. You can frame your questions as follows.

1. What is your opinion about the use of pesticides? Or you may ask,
2. Shall we avoid the use of pesticides?

See another question

Do you use pesticide?

This is a closed form question. So, closed form question requires restricted responses. Such questions will give only superficial information. Open form questions will provide in-depth information

Unstructured Interview: Unstructured or informal type interview is advantageous than the unstructured type as it gives adequate information in depth.

Now we shall see how to develop an interview schedule.

Developing an Interview Schedule

Interview schedule is the written format of items to be asked of the interviewees.

You may have written that the following points are to be considered while developing a schedule. They are fixing the topic framing questions and determining the number and type of questions.

First of all we should identify the purpose of the interview. Thus, you should fix the format of the schedule. Here format means the number of open form and closed form of questions and some introductory questions. The introductory questions will help to establish a rapport between interviewer and interviewee. Then you should frame questions in order to satisfy the purpose of the interview. While framing the questions, you should bear in mind the following aspects:

i) The questions should be simple, clear and straight forward.
ii) Questions should not contain long and confusing statements.
iii) One question should contain only one aspect.
iv) Questions should be stated clearly.

After framing questions you should arrange them in logical order. An illustration for an interview schedule is given as follows.

Illustrative Interview Schedule

An interview schedule to know the attraction of pupils towards TV programmes.

1. What is your name?
2. In which class do you study?
3. How many members are there in your family?
4. Do you have a TV set at your home?
5. Do you see all the Malayalam programmes?
6. Do you see programmes in other languages?
   1. a. Which type of programme do you prefer most?
      b. Why?
   2. a. Which channel programme do you prefer most?
      b. Why?
7. How much time do you spend to watch TV everyday?
   3. a. Do you think that watching TV programmes is very essential?
      b. Why?
   4. a. Do you feel any harm due to watching TV Programmes?
      b. Why?
8. How much time do you spend for studying at home?
   5. a. Do TV programmes negatively affect your study?
      b. Why?
   6. a. Do you think that watching TV will facilitate your study?
      b. How? Why?
   7. Do you have any special suggestions regarding TV programmes?

This is a model format for interviewing pupils. Now we shall see how to conduct an interview.

Conduct of an Interview

Conduct of an interview is a skillful activity. You should follow certain guidelines to conduct an interview. The guidelines are given below:

i) Create a friendly environment for the conduct of interview.
ii) Consider student's responses patiently.
iii) Do not show an authoritarian attitude.
iv) Give enough respect to the interviewee.
v) Do not compel interviewee to give answers as you wish.
vi) Arguments with interviewee should be avoided.
vii) Give positive comments and congratulate interviewee for their good responses.

These are the points to be borne in mind while conducting an interview. These points will help you to conduct the interview successfully.

Sociometry

Sociometric techniques are used to describe the social relationships of an individual in a group and among the members of the group. So, sociometry is a technique to describe acceptance or rejection of individuals among a group. You are familiar with occasions when we ask for students' acceptance to elect a leader or representative for a class. Sociometric technique will help you to identify level of acceptance of each student in your class. Now, let us see how to conduct sociometry.

Conducting Sociometry

Sociometry involves a systematic procedure. Now we will see the details of the procedure. The first step is to identify the acceptance of students in the classroom.

Identification of acceptance level of students: In order to identify the acceptance level of students, you should collect options of every student about all other students. For instance, when a class leader is needed for class you have to use special type of choice forms. Special types of forms should be designed for collecting the options of the students. A choice form should include provision for making three choices namely, first choice, second choice, and third choice. You should direct your students to mark their choice according to the preference to his or her classmates. The choice form should be a piece of paper bearing space to write preference.

You should give necessary instructions to students about how to mark their preference on the choice forms, well before giving the choice forms.

The second step in sociometry is scoring of choice forms.

Scoring of choice forms: You should follow a definite scoring procedure to keep maximum objectivity. Now, you have all forms duly filled in by your students. So let us see how to find out the most preferred and the least preferred students in your class.

The simplest scoring procedure is to count the number of times an individual student is chosen regardless of the order of choice. But this will not give much objectivity. So let us try another procedure for scoring.

You should give convenient points to each choice. Such as, three points to first choice, two points to second choice and one point to third choice. The student who gets maximum score will be the most preferred one in the most preferred individual in a group is termed as the 'star' and the least preferred one in the group is termed as 'neglectee'. An individual who does not choose anybody is termed as an 'isolate'. Now we shall see the final step in sociometry, namely the graphical representation of sociometric data.

Graphic presentation of sociometric data: Now we have the score of sociomatry with the help of which we could construct a very special type of graph namely, the 'sociogram'. This graph will help you to identify the various choice preference of your students and the 'stars'. 'neglectees', and 'isolates'. We shall see the details of preparing a sociogram as follows.

Sociogram

We have already seen that sociogram is the graphical or symbolic representation of sociometric data. There are various symbols that can be used in sociogram.

Other Techniques

We have discussed sociometry and now we are going to discuss two other tools of sociological nature, they are,

a) Guess who technique, and
b) Social distance scale.

Guess who technique

Guess who technique is a simple sociological measurement. In this technique pupils are asked to write the name of individual pupils on the basis of the given explanations. For example, *the statement a vehicle used under sea water is termed as a submarine*, is an explanation for a submarine. Likewise, one should write the name of the pupil from a set of peculiarities. Let us see an example.

1) This boy is the best singer in the class. He is also very good in running and playing football.
2) This girl always quarrels with others.
3) This boy joins with anybody in group activities and helps anyone who needs help.

Likewise you should write statements suitable for each pupil in your class. Many statements should be prepared for each pupil.

Now we shall discuss the scoring process in guess who technique. The scoring procedure is simple. You should give one point (+1) for each good quality marked against a pupil and a negative point (-1) should be given to each bad quality. Then you should add all the plus scores and all the minus scores. The negative scores are then subtracted from the positive scores obtained. The pupils getting highest score have maximum good qualities and those who get lowest score have minimum good qualities.

Social Distance Scale

Social distance is, as the name indicates, a device to measure social distance. Here, social distance means, the extent or degree to which an individual or a group of individual is accepted or rejected by another individual or a group. So this technique will help us to realise the relationships between individual and between groups in a class. Since this device measures the degree of relation, it helps to understand acceptance or rejection among students in a class. The relationship between students can be of three types, such as, complete acceptance where the relationship should be intimate and informal. In partial acceptance, relationship should be formal and in rejection there will not be any relationships. The difference between these three types of relationships can be more clear through the following statements:

1. *I would like to have this one as my best friend (Complete acceptance)*
2. *I would not mind sitting near this fellow (Partial acceptance)*
3. *I wish this student were not in my class (rejection)*

Such statements should be developed and used to measure social distance between your students. You should ask your students to write the name of students as each one consider others, against each statement. You should understand the relationship by consolidating and analysis of responses of all students in the class.

Summing Up

In this chapter we have discussed miscellaneous techniques for evolution such as, analysis of records and documents, interview, sociomatry and other techniques.

1. Analysis of records and documents provides information about attendances, academic achievement, progress in achievement in co-curricular activities, health hobbies.
2. Interview provides valuable information in depth. Interview can be of two types, namely, structured and unstructured with respect to the topic and interviewee.
3. Sociometry is a technique to study social relationship, acceptance or rejection among individuals. Sociogram is the graphical representation of sociometric data.
4. Other techniques such as Guess Who Technique helps to identify individuals possessing maximum good qualities. Social distance scale helps to measure the degree of acceptance of rejection.

Chapter 25
Case Study

Concept of Case Study

Case study is another technique for evaluation. A 'case' may be an individual or a group of individuals, or an institution, as the subject for the study. Case study is the intensive analysis of a case. Case is the centre of the case study. As we are more concerned about teaching, we can use a single individual or a group of individuals as a case.

Identification of a Case

In order to identify an individual as a case, you should observe the case thoroughly, whether s/he is displaying any action requiring special attention. If s/he is showing any symptoms requiring special attention, then we could consider s/he as a case. These symptoms involve serious problems such as isolation, under-achievement, maladjustments, inactivity, hyperactivity, etc.

Isolation

Man is a social animal. Every animal leading a social life will have positive interaction with the members of its community. A person who has very weak connections with other members of the society can be termed as an isolated person. Same type of isolation can be seen among school children also. So, you have to identify such pupils.

Under-achievement

Achievement means level of performance of individual in any type of testing. Usually a teacher will have expectation about the achievement of each of her/his students. A student who is unable to achieve up to this expected level of performance though s/he is able to achieve up to that level is termed as under-achiever, you should locate the under-achievers also.

Maladjustment

Maladjustment in classroom means inability to adjust in classroom situations. These include adjustment problems in sitting in the classroom, in doing learning activities, working with others, etc. So, any maladjustment child can be located immediately.

Inactivity

Our classrooms are heterogenous in nature. So, pupils with difference in abilities can be seen in such classes. Certain students may be very active and rarely one or two inactive pupils also can be seen. You should identify such inactive pupils.

Hyperactivity

Hyperactivity is just opposite of inactivity. A hyperactive pupil will create problems both inside and outside the classroom. Such a pupil cannot engage in an activity patiently. S/he always seems to be disturbed and will try to disturb others. These are the major cues to identify a case. Such hyperactive pupils must be identified.

Steps in Case Study

Analysis of information and suggestions on the basis of the available information are the steps in a case study, after identification of the case.

Locating a Case

Locating a case is otherwise termed as identifying a case. We have already seen the necessary cues for identification of a case. Once we know the symptoms of those who need special attention, then identification process is very easy. What we should do is to observe your pupils closely. Naturally the following questions will arise: what should be observed?, when to observe?, and how to observe?

Observing a child is an easy job. But the important thing is that your observation must be systematic. You should first of all decide what to be observed. You should observe special or exceptional activities and serious problems. In order to know these, you have to observe various activities of students, both inside and outside the classroom and their achievement in curricular and co-curricular activities.

You should keep a record of all pupils. This should involve their grades in examinations, co-curricular activities, their special interest or lack of interest. Cumulative record will help you to locate the probable 'case'.

Collection of Information

Collection of relevant information or data is very crucial as far as a case study is concerned. In order to get relevant information, you should consider the following points:

i) Survey of available sources of information and
ii) Seeking additional information, if necessary

Survey of the sources of information will help you to collect relevant data easily. The major sources of information about a case are observation, informal testing, student's personal folder and records kept by the teacher.

Additional information about pupil's family history, physical and intellectual abilities, emotional patterns, needs, interests and adjustment problems can be obtained by interviewing family members and class mates.

So, observation and interview will help you to collect relevant data of a case. If necessary, appropriate tests / self report also are to be conducted.

Formulation of Hypothesis

You will get a clear picture of student's problem by analysing the collected information. On the basis of this, you should formulate a hypothesis about the problem. Hypothesis is a tentative solution of an identified problem, which can be tested and verified. We shall see an example to make it clear about formulation of hypothesis.

Rajesh is seen inattentive and restless in classroom and he is not able to concentrate in learning activities. From the collected information it is clear that Rajesh has certain problems at his home, responses of teachers also cause adjustment problems. So, a broken home environment and unsuitable attitude of teachers cause defective learning.

Likewise you should make hypothesis of your student's problems on the basis of the identified symptoms.

Design and Try out of Remedial Programme

Once you hypothesis the problem of your students, you should design and try out necessary remedial progammes to solve the problems.

Remedial programmes for each individual pupil should be different from one another, as each one has different problems and different programmes for different cases.

Firstly, you should know the child completely, including his personnel abilities, interests, family history and his problems.

Secondly, you should organise adequate counselling sessions with the pupil. Here counselling involves suggestions and approval of necessary guidelines to overcome the problems.

Thirdly, you should arrange certain practical activities to help your students to overcome their difficulties. Such activities should include provision for participating in group activities, programmes to overcome forgetting, arrangements to avoid seating problems, and programmes to improve study habits.

The most important thing is that you have to design such programmes on the basis of the characteristics of pupils. Now we shall pass on to the fifth step in the case study that is, evaluation of the outcome.

Evaluation of Outcome

At this step you should evaluate whether the programmes used to overcome the problems are effective or not. Observation is very effective for evaluating the programme used to overcome a particular problem. So it is essential to evaluate how far effective the programme used was. Suppose a student is having problem of under achievement, various remedial programmes were used to overcome the problems. Then you should evaluate the effectiveness of the programmes. The evaluation is done by observation and testing. Purposive observation will help you to identify improvements, if any, in your pupil. Along with observation, testing also is helpful to assess changes in achievement. In order to know the changes, you should analyse the progress report of the pupil.

In all other type of problems also, observation of the pupil is the most effective technique to evaluate whether the pupil was able to overcome the problem.

Sometimes progress will not be up to satisfactory level. Then you should design new remedial programmes and re-evaluate the progress. This cycle will be repeated till you get satisfactory progress.

Essential Aspects of a Case Study

We have already discussed the steps in a case study. Now, we shall discuss how to conduct a case study. Certain aspects in conducting a case study are given as follows.

- **i.** ***Long term study***: The first thing to remember is that, case study will take many months to get satisfactory progress. So it is a long term work and you should be well prepared for such a study.
- **ii.** ***Identifying cases***: We have thoroughly discussed how to identify a case and various problems leading to a case. On the basis of those guidelines, you should identify the cases in your classrooms and categorise them as per the nature of problems that they are facing.
- **iii.** ***Develop a healthy attitude***: A healthy attitude should be developed for group activities among the members in the classroom. You should also establish a rapport with the identified cases. You would not directly tell them that they have some problems. On the contrary, you should encourage them to take part in the remedial programme.
- **iv.** ***Develop suitable remedial programme***: You should develop remedial programme suitable for the need and age level of your pupils. Remedial programmes will be simple and directed towards overcoming the problems.
- **v.** ***Seek the help of other pupils***: Peer teaching is very effective. In case study also, we should seek the help of peers for the case in order to assist them to work out remedial programmes.

Case Study — An Illustration

Here we will see the details of the case study, conducted to solve the problems of a secondary school pupil. The example is presented through the same steps as we discussed earlier.

Locating the Case

Som is an eighth standard pupil. In the very first class itself the teacher noted that he was inattentive in the class. After few more classes the teacher made a close observation of Som. The teacher found out that som is silent, disinterested, inattentive and is isolated from other pupils. Now a case is located, so the teacher decided to collect details about Som.

Collection of Information

The teacher observed the 'case' more thoroughly. Along with observation the teacher conducted an interview with the pupil, his mother, other pupils in the class, and had a discussion with other teachers.

All the teachers opined that Som is inactive and disinterested. He does not even respond while they ask questions. His classmates brought out the fact that Som has no friends in the class and in any other classes. They also said that Som was unwilling to speak freely with them. He always showed shyness when others tried to keep his company. Som's mother said he is the youngest of her children and did not know how to talk with others and behave properly. The teacher reminded the mother that Som is a fourteen year old, and he is able to take decisions by himself. The mother was surprised to hear it and said Som is the baby in their home and he is unable to do anything as the teacher said.

Som, in response to the informal interview said that though he is grown up in age and size, his parents and siblings consider him as a small child. They are always behind him with so many dont's. So he gradually developed into an isolate, mainly because of shyness and confusion about other's responses towards his behaviour.

Formulation of Hypothesis

A thorough analysis of the information obtained from these sources bring out the clear picture of Som's problems, which can be hypothesised as follows.

Lack of adequate social interaction leads to isolation, and is thereby causing problems in learning.

Design and Try out of Remedial Programmes

The teacher organised the following remedial programmes such as counselling session with the pupil and his parents and practical activities to overcome problems of the pupil.

Counselling session with the pupil was directed towards developing his self confidence. Teacher gave necessary direction for Som's parents to treat him as a young man and provide opportunity to his self development. To making him participate in decision-making discussions at home, entrust him the responsibility of certain home affairs, and to stop scolding him as a small child, were suggested by the teacher.

Teacher advised other pupils in the class to mingle with Som so that he could overcome his shyness.

Teachers also planned certain group activities to facilitate learning. Activities such as selecting him as the leader of the group, once he became an active member of a group.

Evaluation of Outcome

After a few weeks the teacher evaluated the outcome of the remedial programmes that he adopted in his class. There was marked change in the behaviour of Som and his classroom achievements. This shows that the remedial programmes helped him to overcome his problems. Evaluation was done by observation and achievement test.

The remedial programmes were organised for some more time to overcome the problems of Som completely.

Summing Up

In this chapter we have discussed the details of case study. Case Study is an in-depth study of an individual or a group of individuals or an institution, which is termed as a 'case'. A case can be identified on the basis of symptoms such as isolation, under-achievement, maladjustment, inactivity, hyper activity, etc.

The steps in case study are:

a) Identification of a case
b) Collection of information
c) Formulation of hypothesis
d) Design and try out of remedial programme and
e) Evaluation of outcome

The essential aspects of a case study are as follows:

i) It is a long term study
ii) Identification of case is important
iii) Develop healthy attitude for group work among pupils
iv) Development of suitable remedial programmes
v) Seek help of other pupils

Chapter 26
Scoring and Grading

SCORING

Concept

Scoring is a very familiar process for all of us. Scoring is the integral part of teaching, as it is a part of evaluation. Scoring means making the score of each item in an evaluation tool. You are familiar with scoring of achievement tests. The score in a test means the total score obtained for a particular student in that test. So score is the technical term for marks, and scoring is assigning marks to the responses of individual students for each question or item. In scoring you should evaluate the correctness of responses of students according to questions given to them.

Steps in Scoring

Scoring procedure begins at the time of question paper setting of an achievement test. The same is the case of scoring of other types of evaluation tools also. But, as far as our daily use is concerned, we should concentrate the scoring of an achievement test. The first step of scoring is planning.

Planning for Scoring

We know that planning is essential for the success of any activity, so a thorough planning is essential for accurate scoring also. Planning should begin at the time of selection of objective and specification and the question. Development of scoring key and marking scheme is the results of such planning. So the development of scoring key and marking scheme is the second step in scoring.

Development of scoring key and marking scheme

Scoring key can be the key meant for scoring the objective type questions. Such scoring key involves question numbers, alphabets representing correct answers, and score for each answer.

GRADING

Usually after scoring you should communicate the score of each student in the classroom. As per the present system, those who get thirty five per cent marks will pass in the examination. So, one student who got thirty five out of hundred and other one who got sixty out of hundred respectively have passed in the examination. We can make only quantitative difference among the two. If we want to express the difference qualitatively we should change the mode of communication. Here comes the importance of grading. Now we shall discuss the meaning, bases, and procedure of grading.

Meaning

Usually we use progress reports to communicate student's progress. But progress report does not serve the actual function of communicating results. Through the progress report, you do not convey details of the performance of a student, such as how good or bad the student performs. Here comes the importance of grading.

Grading means describing a student's performance qualitatively using symbols. Here qualities involve the level of performance of individuals in an achievement test. For example, grading will help us to describe "how good" or "how bad" one performs in an achievement test. The symbols used can be some of the first letters in English, such as A, B, C, D and E. Grading will help us to make precise judgement of one's performance also.

In grading we use narrow range scale as against the wide range scale we used in an achievement test. That is an achievement test, may be designed with a maximum marks of fifty or hundred. On the contrary, a grading scale will be very narrow, with five or seven grade points use symbols such as A, B, C, D and E in a five point scale the grade point and performance level in each as follows.

Grade Point	Letter Grade	Level of Performance
5	A	Excellent
4	B	Very good
3	C	Good
2	D	Satisfactory
1	E	Unsatisfactory

You can further lengthen the scale to a seven point scale or a nine point scale, by using additional symbols such as A+, B+ and C+, as we are familiar in the present evaluation system.

In order to attain each grade point, one must have attained certain standards of performance. And now we shall pass on to the bases of grading.

Bases of Grading

There are different bases of grading. The bases of grading mean the standards used for describing a grade, that is the level of performance such as good or average or poor. Such description of the performance is based on some standards. You should either take the performance of the whole class as a standard or consider an ideal level of performance. So there are two bases of grading such as,

i. Relative grading standards (consider the performance of whole group as the standard)
ii. Absolute grading standard (An ideal level of performance as the standard)

Relative grading standard: In relative grading standard, grading is done according to the rank of a learner in relation to the other learners of the same class. But, you only rank your students and not grade them. In relative grade you should specify group learners with a selected level of percentage of performance as a grade. Scales with five points or seven points or nine points can be used in this type of grading.

Absolute grading standards: In absolute grading standards, each grade can be attained by achieving a set of scores. So in order to attain a grade, we should achieve the prescribed set of scores. In another form, a given quantum of content or level of mastery of given skills is to be achieved to attain a concerned grade.For example, a student should be awarded 'A' grade, if he/she is able to answer correctly all the essential aspects of nervous co-ordination in an achievement test.

Procedure of Grading

At the time of grading, you should first of all look for the different item types, such as objective type, and free response type, because scales of different range will be suitable for different item types.

In evaluating an objective type item, the answer can be either right or wrong. So, a two point scale is essential for evaluating an objective type item. The two point scale can be 0-1, when 1 stands for correct response and '0' stands for wrong response.

But evaluation of short answer type question requires a scale with more than two points. A three point scale may be serving the purpose of evaluating a short answer type item. So the scale can be 0-3, where '3' stands for a good answer, '2' stands for a moderately good answer and '0' for a wrong answer.

In evaluating an essay type answer, you should consider a fairly long scale; usually a seven point scale will serve this purpose. So the scale can be 0-6, each grade point can be as follows.

6	-	Outstanding
5	-	Very good
4	-	Good
3	-	Average
2	-	Fair
1	-	Poor
0	-	Failure

In grading an essay type item, you should consider adequacy, appropriateness and relevance of the context, clarity of form, imagination and resourcefulness of the presentation.

Here you should note one thing that, scales with different grade points are used to grade different item types in the same test. Our aim is to grade the student on the basis of the achievement test. So you should combine grades of different item types to get the comprehensive grade of the achievement test. In order to get an accurate grade, you should standardise the grade points into a common scale. You should select a scale as the standard, and scores on other scales should be converted to that scale.

Summing Up

a. In this chapter we have discussed the details of scoring and grading. Scoring is marking the score of items in an evaluation tool. Grading is the symbolic representation of students' performance qualitatively.
b. Planning for scoring and development of scoring key and marking scheme are the steps in scoring.
c. Relative grading standard and absolute grading standard are the bases of grading.
d. There are different scales for grading different item types. But all these scales should be standardised to a single scale. Grade for a single subject, all subjects, terminal examination and annual grade can be calculated using different formula.

CHAPTER 27

Diagnostic Testing and Remedial Teaching

Diagnostic testing and remedial teaching are the essential parts of evaluation.

DIAGNOSTIC TESTING

Diagnostic testing is an old concept included in evaluation. But it is a neglected part of evaluation. Actually diagnostic testing is a very essential part of evaluation which helps the learner to learn more easily and the teacher to teach effectively. So, we shall discuss the meaning, purpose, planning, developing and administrating of a diagnostic test in detail as follows.

Meaning of Diagnostic Testing

'Diagnosis' is a familiar term for us, because clinical diagnosis of various diseases is familiar to all of you. The term diagnostic testing means the testing for revealing specific weakness of difficulties. This is the general meaning of a diagnosis test. Now we shall think of the meaning of diagnostic testing as far as classroom teaching is concerned. Here, diagnostic testing is testing meant for revealing weaknesses and difficulties in learning and thereby in achievement. Diagnostic test is a specially designed test to reveal the specific weaknesses and difficulties in learning and which lead to under-achievement. Here, under achievement means not achieving up to the expected level, though the student is able to achieve up to that level. Naturally diagnostic test should be conducted at any time requiring diagnosis of weaknesses or difficulties in learning. An achievement test itself can be converted to a diagnostic test, so as to locate the areas of difficulties. But in a diagnostic test a small piece of content is taken and as many questions as possible are developed from it.

Planning and Developing a Diagnostic Test

Planning is the first step of diagnostic testing also. At the planning stage, you should determine the scope, nature, level and time schedule of the test. The scope of the test involves the nature and type of weaknesses and difficulties that might have happened during the leaning of the given content. You should anticipate the probable errors and have to determine the level and outline of content, on the basis of which the diagnostic test is to be developed. The important thing is that only a small content area should be included in a diagnostic test. An achievement test also could be considered as a diagnostic test if it involves a small portion of content and maximum questions from it.

Then you should determine the time schedule and duration of test. The time schedule may be the period assigned for the selected subject or a specific time selected according to your convenience. But duration of the test may not be limited, i.e., enough time should be given to your pupils to answer all the questions.

The steps in developing a diagnostic test have certain similarities to that of an achievement test. The steps in developing an achievement test were discussed earlier in this unit. The steps of conducting diagnostic testing are fixing instructional objectives, design of blue print, writing of questions, administering the test and development of diagnostic chart.

Preparation of Diagnostic Chart and Diagnosing Weaknesses

Diagnostic chart is a specially designed chart used for analysing the responses of each student against each question. Such an analysis is used to diagnose the weaknesses or difficulties in learning the given content. Now, we shall discuss the different elements of a diagnostic chart.

Elements of diagnostic chart: The major elements of diagnostic chart are as follows:

a) Name of pupils (Total number of pupils who attended the test).
b) Type of question (Objective type, short answer type and essay type).
c) Responses of each student to each question.
d) Total number of correct answers, wrong answers, partially correct answers, and omitted questions.
e) Total marks and remarks (whether passed or failed) obtained by each student.
f) A consolidated table including the total number of students responded correctly, wrongly, partially correctly and omitted question.

In a diagnostic chart, there should be a separate row for each student and separate column for each question. This is because you have to note down the details of responses of each student to each item in the appropriate column. Then only you can diagnose difficulties.

1. The students who are able to respond correctly for most of the questions.
2. Students who are unable to respond well.
3. The question / questions which are answered by most of the students.

4. The question/questions which are difficult to be answered, unanswered and wrongly answered.
5. The areas posing difficulty to all the pupils.
6. Students having weakness at special areas.

REMEDIAL TEACHING

Remedial teaching is a concept that stands in close relation with diagnostic testing. That is, remedial teaching comes just after diagnostic testing. Along with mastery learning that we have seen in the concept of remedial teaching. Now we shall see the meaning and conduct of remedial teaching.

Meaning of Remedial Teaching

Remedial teaching is the special programme used to remove the weakness in learning and thereby achievement.

Usually we are teaching our students and evaluating them periodically. But after valuing the answer papers and communicating the scores of each student, you may naturally pass on to the next topic or chapter. Sometimes, you may discuss the question paper in the classroom and proceed to the next chapter. So, naturally those ideas which are not learned properly, will remain as such and it creates a gap in learning. Definitely this will affect further learning. Here comes the importance of remedial teaching.

Remedial teaching helps you to organise suitable programmes to bridge the gap in learning by making necessary changes in teaching or learning programme. It also helps to remove unnecessary or unwanted habits and attitude needed for optimum learning. So naturally a question will arise, that, how do we know the desirable habits, skills and attitude needed for optimum learning? Thorough analysis of habits skills and attitude required for learning at such a level help us to understand the competence required for optimum performance.

Organising Remedial Teaching

We have discussed how to diagnose the weaknesses and difficulties in learning and teaching. Now, we can see the details of organising remedial teaching. At first we will see the detailed steps of organising remedial teaching.

Planning

The planning is the first step of any organised form of activity. So, before you (teacher) begin with remedial teaching session, plan thoroughly the various aspects of remedial teaching.

At first, identify the areas in which pupils felt difficulty. This will help in makng use of suitable remedial measures.

Secondly, you have to determine the nature and type of difficulties that require special assistance from your side. Generally, incomplete learning misses representation of concepts, concepts not properly developed, etc. might be some of the difficulties that may have occured in learning and teaching in your classroom.

Thirdly, you have to identify the number of students who committed errors in answering each question. You should also analyse the type of errors each one made while answering. So, you should get an overall view of the errors as well as the errors made by each student.

Then you should determine the nature and type of remedial programmes which are required in removing weaknesses or difficulties in teaching and learning that occurred previously.

Finally, you should evaluate the effectiveness of the remedial measures adopted to remove the weakness and difficulties in teaching and learning. This should be done with the help of periodical questioning / testing.

Design of Remedial Teaching

Once you have identified the weaknesses and difficulties in teaching and learning, you should develop suitable remedial measures.

You should utilise special programmes in this regard. These programmes can be of the following nature:

- Alternative instructional methods and learning activities.
- Use more accessory learning materials to get clarity for each concept.
- Give enough time for mastery over the given content. (because aptitude is a function of time).
- Employ review at the points wherever necessary. This will help the learners to know their progress and help the teachers to know the level of learning.

So in essence, you should utilise a new method / methods for instructing the given content, as the instructional procedure depends on the nature of the content.

A variety of accessory learning materials can be used to facilitate learning. You can also ask your students to prepare certain accessory learning materials. This will help their interest in learning. All these aspects connected with accessory learning aids are discussed earlier in connection with other relevant content areas. So it is unnecessary to discus all these aspects in detail once again.

Summing Up

We have discussed the details of diagnostic testing and remedial teaching. Diagnostic testing means testing to know the difficulties and weaknesses in learning a given content.

Diagnostic testing involves fixing of instructional objectives, design of blue print, writing questions, testing and development of a diagnostic chart.

Diagnostic chart involves name of pupils, type of questions, responses of each student, total number and types of responses, and total marks obtained for each student are also presented.

Remedial teaching means special teaching programme used to remove weaknesses and difficulties in learning thereby ensuring achievement.

While organising remedial teaching, alternative teaching methods and additional learning aids should be used. Enough time should be given to get mastery. Periodic assessment should be conducted to ensure progress.

CHAPTER 28
Self Evaluation

Evaluating yourself is an essential part of your teaching, because self evaluation will help you to improve your teaching. Increase in quality of teaching results in better teaching. At the same time, self evaluation helps you for your personal development also.

Self Evaluation Concept

Self evaluation is a traditional concept, which is practised very rarely. Self evaluation means evaluating the effectiveness of an individual by oneself. In the case of a teacher, s/he should evaluate own teaching efficiency and performance. Of course there are systematic methods and procedure for self evaluation. Such self evaluation methods will help you to improve yourself. In addition to individual development, self evaluation influences other teachers in your school and has influence on teachers in other institutions also. Thus, self evaluation creates a motive towards improving instructional processes. Self evaluation also helps you to assess yourself without the knowledge of other teachers, if you wanted so. That is, you can keep your weaknesses as a secret and develop steps to eliminate such weaknesses.

In another way, self evaluation means evaluating yourself with the help of other teachers or students or by self. Techniques such as observation with rating scales, checklists, etc. can be used to evaluate your teaching with the help of other teachers. Such rating will give you a more precise report of your performance and abilities. If you evaluate yourself with the help of students, you should give necessary direction to them, and do not tell them openly, that they are going to evaluate you.

In essence, self evaluation means evaluation of your teaching competence in one way or the other with or without the help of others.

Purposes of Self Evaluation

Now we shall discuss about 'why' of self evaluation in some more detail. In order to answer this 'why', we shall analyse the purposes of self evaluation. The most important purposes of self evaluation are as follows:

- Assessment and assistance.
- Individual improvement

- Professional development
- School improvement

Assessment and Assistance of Teachers

One of the basic functions of evaluation is assessing and assisting teachers, especially beginners. Beginning teachers may have different problems in teaching. So it is essential to assess their difficulties and give necessary professional assistance. You may be familiar with the difficulties of beginners in teaching.

You may have suggested the following difficulties such as unfamiliarity with actual classroom situation, students, instructional activities, accessory learning materials, classroom management, and conduct of evaluation. Usually beginner will have difficulty to understand the effect of his/ her teaching on students and their extent of learning. The role of assessment and assistance is highly essential at this beginning stage. So evaluation provides necessary directions to beginners.

Individual Improvement

Another important purpose of self evaluation is individual improvement. That is improvement of performance. Evaluation helps to understand problems in performance and strategies, and to develop suitable remedial programmes. Such remedial programmes will help you to improve your teaching performance.

Professional Development

Professional development is another basic purpose of self evaluation. This involves collection of data to determine the extent to which teachers have achieved minimum acceptance levels of competence and performance standards. Collection of data will be helpful to assist teachers who have minimum level of competence to develop further. Professional development can occur in the following five areas.

i) Instruction – The development of skills involved with instruction technology, courses media, etc.
ii) Professional – growth of an individual in professional roles (i.e. as a teacher)Organisational – growth in identifying needs, priorities and organisation of the institution
iii) Career – preparation for career advancement
iv) Personal –planning for professional growth, interpersonal skills, etc.

Professional development is very important since most of the teachers seem to desire it.

School Improvement

Professional development of teachers will contribute to school improvement. Such professional could be able to develop programmes for improving school instruction. This can be attained only through evaluation of professional competence and adopting suitable remedial measures. Thus, school improvement also becomes a purpose of self evaluation.

These are the purposes of self evaluation. Before we pass on to the next section please check your progress in this chapter.

Methods of Self Evaluation

Now we shall discuss the different methods of evaluation. The important methods are observation, extended observation and self assessment.

Observation

We have already discussed different observational techniques for evaluating our students. Self evaluation can be done using observation with the help of other teachers or experts in the field of observation. Naturally a question will arise as to what should be observed?

Certain essential aspects of instructional activity should be observed to evaluate your competence. Those aspects include teacher activity, pupil activity, instructional media used, use of accessory learning materials, classroom climate, classroom management, periodical review, etc.

How do we observe the essential aspects of classroom instruction? Observation can be done with the help of a special format, which is prepared well in advance. Such a format should involve all the essential aspects to be observed. This type of observation can be termed as closed system of observation. Observation can be done without such a special format. Here the observer marks what he had seen in the classroom and makes a summary of his observation. This type of observation can be termed as closed system of observation.

In closed type observation system checklists or behaviour categories can be used to mark observation. We have already discussed observational checklists. Such checklists are the easiest and suitable device to make the observation and finally a summary of generalised suggestions for improvement.

Extended Observation

Extended observation means observation with the help of rating scales. A rating scale is used to measure how well or bad is one's performance in different aspects of an activity, here instruction. This is done by providing different points for each aspect. For example, the points can be very poor

/poor/ average/ good/ excellent in a five point scale. You can make a list of teacher activities in the classroom and mark your responses on the right point of scale.

Self Assessment

Self assessment is the most useful method of evaluating your teaching behaviour, instructional strategies and techniques. The rate of improvement by this method will be greater than that of other methods used for evaluation because, in self assessment you feel your difficulties and weaknesses. We can use the following three steps for increasing the effectiveness of self assessment.

a) Identification of present teaching behaviour
b) Identification of problem areas and weaknesses in present teaching
c) Elimination of problems and weaknesses and adopting to a new teaching behaviour

Then you should evaluate the new behaviour for its effectiveness. So the process of self assessment is ongoing and unending, directed towards one's professional development to its maximum.

There are different techniques for self assessment. Now let us see the important techniques for self assessment.

Techniques of Self Assessment: There is a variety of techniques for self assessment such as video or audio feedback, self rating forms, self reports, comparison to standards, self study materials and students' achievement. Let us see each of these in detail.

Video or audio feed back: This technique involves the recording of the teaching either in video tape or in audio tape. Here the purpose of recording is self assessment. This type of recording helps you to view or to hear your own teaching and to understand the weaknesses of your teaching. This will be the best objective feed back of your teaching. Such recording will also help you to improve your teaching competence up to a greater extent. Audio tape is cheaper than video tape and easily available for you. So you can use audiotapes for recording your teaching.

Self rating forms: Self rating form is just like a rating scale, which involves a variety of teaching skills listed in logical order. You should use rating scales in the same fashion of rating scales for students. Rating scales of this type are simply checklists of specific teaching behaviours, frequency of behaviours and sequence of behaviours. Here you should rate your own behaviours from memory in the list provided in the self rating forms after teaching. We have discussed rating scales in detail in Chapter 3 of this unit.

Self reports: Self reports resemble self rating forms, as it demands your response against a predetermined format. But the format of self report forms consists of open ended questions related to instruction. This device helps you to evaluate your teaching behaviours, aims, priorities, and shortcomings. These forms should be clear, brief and should be used on a regular basis i.e. at least once in a month. Now let us see some statements that should be included in self reports.

A. Whether the aims of teaching this content are realised?
B. Have I covered all the priority areas in a given content?
C. Did I think the prerequisites required for the instruction with the given content appropriate?
D. Did I utilise all media suitable for effective instruction of the content?
E. What was the nature of learning activities? Are they effective?
F. Could I utilise all the useful accessory learning materials for instruction?
G. How was the evaluation of instruction of the given content organised?

You should leave enough space after each question, so that the responses against each should be written in that space. At the end you should get a complete account of your own teaching.

Comparison to standards: Observation of high quality (standard) teaching to realise the standard of teaching is the basis of this technique. Once you are familiar with the establish standard then you can compare your teaching with the established standard. Through this technique, you will be able to identify the shortcomings in your teaching and improve your teaching.

Self study materials: Self study materials are specially designed materials which helps you to assess or analyse your teaching style. For example, in a self study material a teacher gets details of a new method of instruction for a given content. Naturally you will get a chance to compare your approaches with the one given in the material. So, you could understand the advantages of the new approach and you can adopt them. Thus, self study materials also help you in self assessment. This self instructional package is an example for this method.

Student's achievement: Student's achievement can be considered as a device of self assessment. This is a very easy technique for self evaluation, because our instruction aims at behavioural changes in students. If your students can achieve highly, then your instruction may be of good quality. If your students are not able to perform well in achievement tests, then you could infer that there exist certain shortcomings in your teaching. In this sense, student's achievement can be considered as an index of self assessment. For example, Rahul has ninety per cent and above marks in all subjects except social science in which he has only forty per cent marks. Naturally, we will go through the marks of other students in social science. Surprisingly, all students have secured low marks in social science. So we could infer that there exist certain problems in the teaching of social science.

So, on the basis of student's achievement you could analyse various aspects of your teaching, and be able to improve yourself. These are the various techniques for self assessment.

Summing Up

In this chapter we have discussed the details of self evaluation. Self evaluation is necessary to remove weakness in teaching. The purposes of self evaluation are:

1. Assessment and assistance of teachers
2. Individual improvement
3. Professional development
4. School improvement

There are various methods for self evaluation, such as, observation, extended observation and self assessment. Different techniques for self assessment are:

1. Video or audio feed back
2. Self rating forms
3. Self reports
4. Comparison to standards
5. Self study materials
6. Student's achievement

UNIT 7
Classroom Management

CHAPTER 29

Aspects of Classroom Management

Educational institutions can be generally categorised into different groups on the basis of management as government, government aided, self financing institutions; on the basis of location, such as rural, urban, coastal, etc. We know that the students belonging to all these areas are enrolled in institutions in their own locality. We also have English medium schools and school with the regional language as the medium of instruction. Students belonging to each of such types of schools have peculiar discipline problems. So, as teachers, it is our duty to understand the discipline problems in students which influence classroom management. The development stage of discipline, characteristics of teacher, and classroom climate have influence on classroom management.

Meaning

Management is the sum total of activities that a manager does in order to obtain better product in an enterprise. In this sense, we teachers also have a managerial role, that is the classroom management. Classroom management stands for management of various activities in the classroom in order to optimise learning. You are familiar with various activities that are organised for learning. Usually you have planned those activities in relation to the topic, level of students and facilities available for learning. Since, classroom activities are meant for maximum learning it is essential to know the factors influencing classroom activities. You should know about discipline, characteristics of teachers, classroom climate and influence of these on classroom management. On the basis of these aspects you can develop a better plan of action and be able to organise it well. Then you will be able to manage classroom activities better than you have done earlier.

Discipline and Classroom Management

Discipline influences classroom management to a greater extent. So it is essential to know the concept of discipline, and the stages of development of discipline, to tackle well with disciplinary problems and to have a better classroom management.

Concept of Discipline

Discipline is one of the concepts we usually misinterpret, as in the case of personality. Now try to examine the meaning of the discipline. Usually teachers will have discussions in the staff room about students of different classes. You may say 'X-B is a worse class, the students are not disciplined'. Other teachers will also support your opinion. Here, what do you mean by discipline? Simply obedience and orderly conduct. It is not discipline that we mean to achieve through education. You mean that students of X B classes were making noise, passing unnecessary comments, raising unwanted questions, etc. while you are teaching. We all think that children must keep quite, when we are talking. To certain extent it is correct, because it will help them to be more attentive. But this is a type of 'obey the order' discipline, which is not suitable for the purpose of education.

The discipline which we mean is *'the dynamic self directing process, by which children are responsible to direct energy towards learning goals'*. When the teacher makes them simply obey, they will be afraid of generating suggestions or asking doubts. But in self directive process, they themselves are responsible for learning, so there may not be the question of fear. For example, you are going to teach diffusion. You take a beaker with water and add one drop of ink to it. Then ask your students to observe and report what is happening? And why is it happening so? Here, your students will generate ideas of their own, and explore the truth, though they are a bit noisy. So discipline is a self directive process leading to learning goals regardless of noise produced or not. Our duty is to help our students to use and develop this self directive process.

Stages of Discipline

We have already discussed the various stages of development in Unit 1. And now, we are going to discuss about the stages of discipline. On the basis of the theories of Piaget and Kohlberg, three stages of development of discipline are put forward. These stages are meant to give a guideline to students and teachers of what to do to foster development of discipline. The stages are as follows:

1. Basic disciplinary stage,
2. Constructive stage, and
3. Generating stage.

Now let us examine the important responsibilities of students and role of teachers at each stage.

Stage 1. Basic Disciplinary Stage: This is the first and the basic stage of discipline. This stage is the characteristic feature of those who come to school first in their life without any home training. The classroom environment will be new to the children. So, they will not know how to behave properly in such a set up. A child, who is first brought to a classroom, will take some time or days or months to adopt to the new environment.

Now let us see what the role of the teachers is at this stage.

a. You should give necessary directions to your pupilsFor example, you are facing a group of first standard students, *you should address them as 'I am your teacher, my name is .... and I am residing at ....*
now tell me your name one by one,
so all of you should heard the name of others..................
you should stand up and greet the teachers when they come into the class.
You should bring your books from tomorrow onwards............ 'and so on goes the list of directions. You should give the directions precisely and clearly at the right time.

b. Encourage your students to ask their doubts and questions

Our students will have many doubts and questions at this stage. So it is our duty to encourage them in doing so, rather than scolding them. For example, one of your students asks "*Why do we wear uniform?*". "*Listen students you must do what I say*". This answer is not appropriate because it is better to give the rationale of any doubt raised by students. So you should say "*Look students, there are rich people and poor people but we consider all of you alike. If you wear coloured dress, many of you have good dress and some of you have only one or two dresses which might cause discrimination among you. That is why we decided that all of you should wear uniform*".

So, at this stage, students should listen to and follow the directions given by teachers and to ask questions about their doubts.

Stage II Constructive stage: The children, after completing the development of basic disciplinary stage, will pass on to the second stage, namely the constructive stage.

The students at this stage are able to perform constructive activities in the classroom. They should work co-operatively with his classmates and are able to exchange or share ideas between them. So they have a leading role in determining the nature of discipline of the classroom.

Now let us see what the teacher should do at this stage.

i. You should provide opportunities to your students to work together co-operatively. In this regard you should encourage your students to participate in group activities such as project work, group investigation, group discussion, cultural activities and field trip.

While taking part in the organisation and execution of such activities, students should get an opportunity for further development through a constructive stage of discipline.

ii. Teacher should give necessary guidance:

iii. Necessary guidance should be given to your students during the conduct of group activities. Because each student should know his role in the activity, and how his performance affects others. These two are the minimum requirements for a democratic society. So you should help your students to understand their role and duties. Now, we shall pass on to the next stage of development of discipline, generative stage, by which we could lead our students to the highest level of discipline.

Stage III Generative stage: The students at this stage have more initiative in social responsibilities than students at constructive stage. For example, *suppose we are exposed to an accident site. An injured man is lying on the road. A crowd around him is watching. A person who is at the highest stage of discipline will take necessary steps to help the injured man. But others will be still in doubt about the police case and such affairs.*

Students at generative stage will show such a leadership as in the previous example. They will stand for justice. They can understand the problems in the society and generate solutions for those problems. So, by the completion of development of this stage, a student should become an enlightened citizen, that is a citizen who always searches for duties than rights. They can also take a right and fight position against conflicts in life.

Now let us see the role of teachers in the generative stage of discipline. At this stage also you should provide leadership opportunities to your students. For example, you make a plan for a field trip and ask your students to make necessary arrangements. The students will get enough opportunity for social responsibility, leadership and problem solving. You must give necessary suggestions to your students as and when required.

Now it is clear that classroom discipline is influenced greatly by the stages of development of discipline. So you have to understand the stages of discipline before analysing the disciplinary problems in students. So, it is your duty to provide adequate activities to students in accordance with their developmental stage of discipline. If the students do not get opportunity for proper development of discipline, there will be disciplinary problems. Such disciplinary problems in turn result in improper classroom management.

Characteristics of Teacher and Classroom Management

Characteristics of teacher is another aspect influencing classroom management. Since the role of the teacher is very important in having a better classroom management. It is essential to know the role of the teacher and characteristics of outstanding teachers. First of all, we shall see the role of the teacher.

Role of the Teacher

You have to perform a twin role in maintaining classroom management. This twin role involves factors influenced by teachers and factors controlled by teachers. That is, a teacher shall influence certain factors, and teacher can control some other factors. Both of these together contribute to the effective role of a teacher and thereby better classroom management. Now, let us see the details of the role of a teacher.

1. *Factors influenced by teachers*: The major factors influenced by teachers are parent teacher relationships, out of school aspects and administrative aspects. These factors are called teacher influenced factors, because teacher can only influence these factors and not able to control them.

In this regard, you should take chances to know the parents personally and their attitude. You may have experienced many aggressive parents in your teaching life. If you patiently listen to their opinion, they may be willing to listen to you later. Another thing you should do is to include pupils in parent teacher meetings, which will help you in the management discipline. If it is not possible, you should arrange a pupil teacher meeting, just before parent teacher meeting.

Out of school aspects include nature of homework, home environment, and influence of media on students. Here also the teacher can gather relevant information regarding these aspects from parents and is only able to give suggestions. Administrative aspects include observation of national days and festivals, conduct of co-curricular activities such as sports meet, youth festival, excursion, science fair and so on. A teacher can only influence these aspects as they are joint ventures and therefore only propose one's suggestions.

Now we shall pass on to the factors controlled by teachers.

2. *Factors controlled by teachers*: There are factors which a teacher can control to some extent. Major among such factors are instruction, classroom management and evaluation. Methods and materials utilised for instruction will have influence on classroom management. So, approach in instruction and evaluation should be designed in such a way to avoid disciplinary problems. You (teacher) should have adequate control over the instructional process and means of evaluation. You should also design your own approach in classroom management. So, in all these aspects

teacher is the ultimate authority responsible for the activities to be organised in the classroom, hence we term these as factors controlled by teachers.

Teacher characteristics have profound influence on the role of the teacher, as one's characteristics determine better performance. In order to make this clear, we shall see the characteristics of outstanding teachers, as these characteristics help for better classroom management.

Characteristics of Outstanding Teachers

Let us recollect our teachers who taught us from first standard to higher education level. Can you name all of them? Or could you remember even the face of all of them? If you are lucky, you will remember at least few of them, because of their outstanding characteristics and performance.

You may have remember the following major characteristics such as a teacher should be,

- Well qualified.
- Excellent in communication.
- An expert in teaching using different methods, and
- Always consider the interests of students.

In addition to these, we can identify certain other characteristics as follows.

The teacher will be:

- Warm, understanding and friendly.
- Responsible and systematic.
- Stimulative and considerate to pupils.
- Approachable and communicative.
- Always fair, smart and well prepared.
- Have empathy for students and skilled in various aspects of teaching.

These are the major characteristics of outstanding teachers. These characteristics will help a teacher to perform the role effectively. Effective role-performance of a teacher is necessary for better classroom management. If the characteristics and thereby the behaviour of the teacher is not up to the mark, there will be problems in classroom management.

Suppose, Raj is a secondary school teacher, who does not posses outstanding characteristics. He acts as the sole authority to determine overall activities of the class. He always prefers lecture and recitation methods of teaching. Naturally problems in classroom management are common in Raj's class.

Now, let us have a look at Ms. Julie's class. The teacher co-operates with her students in organising various activities in the class. She acts as a facilitator of students' activities. She always gives necessary guidelines to her students. These good characteristics of teacher create the feeling of oneness among her students. They are highly responsible and generative. So, problems in classroom management never occur in her class. From these examples, it is clear that characteristics of a teacher have high influence on classroom management.

Classroom Climate and Classroom Management

Climate is a familiar term, but classroom climate may be an unfamiliar one. Climate means, almost all aspects of climatic changes on environment and living beings.

Classroom climate also has similar features of environmental climate such as warmth, cold, etc. A warm classroom will give acceptance to students and make them feel secure.

A cold classroom climate is the one that threatens students and make them feel insecure and fearful. Proper learning can happen in a classroom with warm climate only. So classroom climate means the emotional set up prevailing in the classroom that influences learning.

The factors determining the nature of classroom climate are degree of formality, flexibility, structure of class, anxiety, teacher control and stimulation. All these factors contribute classroom climate. Now, let us discuss these factors in detail.

Factors of Classroom Climate

The various factors involved in classroom climate are discussed as follows.

- *Degree of formality*: Formality is a familiar term. In our daily life we have to show formality at many occasions. Here, degree of formality means the degree of relationship between teacher and pupils. Let us remember our teachers, some of them might be informal and they should have had a very good relationship with students. So degree of formality means, how far formal is the teacher in the classroom. Highly formal in class is not suitable for developing good discipline in classroom.
- *Flexibility and structure of classroom:* Flexibility and structure of classroom are related factors. So, we shall discuss these two together. In certain classes teacher adopts a particular teaching method or assigns a particular activity to all students regardless of their ability. Many of them may not follow the teacher or could not do the activity successfully. Hence, the teacher should adopt another method of teaching or

suggest any other activity that can help the children properly. Here, by suggesting alternative activities, the teacher makes the situation flexible. If the teacher does not do so, learning will be impossible and disciplinary problems may arise. Thus, flexibility means provision of alternative situations or activities for facilitating learning.

You will normally prepare a lesson plan or plan of activities before teaching a lesson. In certain situations, as we mentioned in the case of flexibility, you have to deviate from your teaching plan to a certain extent. You have to develop the lesson through a series of activities, structured well in advance. The structuring may be very high, if you have not deviated from your teaching plan. So, structure of classroom means predetermination of activities that should happen in the classroom. But a classroom which is moderately structured, or low structured alone contributes to productive classroom climate thereby will be a disciplined class.

- *Anxiety, teacher control and stimulation*: Now we shall discuss the three factors anxiety, teacher control and stimulation, which are dependent on the factors already discussed such as formality, flexibility, and structure. Let us see what is the meaning of each factor and how these relate to the factors discussed earlier.

Anxiety is a psychological process, which is exhibited by almost all individuals during stressful situation. The degree of anxiety depends on the nature of the individuals. In class room situations, teacher and structure of classroom influence anxiety in children. If the teacher is informal and classroom is low structured, the degree of anxiety will be reduced.

As teachers, all of you should supervise activities of students during the learning process, in order to facilitate learning. This teacher control, to a certain extent, is good for productive classroom climate. But too much control is not productive. So try to exert minimum control while your students are learning.

In your daily teaching, you should stimulate your students for learning. For stimulating them you may narrate incidents, show specimens, ask them to contribute their views and encourage them for answering your questions. Such stimulative activities are very essential for a productive classroom climate and is dependent on the will of the teacher. We have discussed various factors of a classroom climate. And now we shall discuss about certain points to be borne is mind for establishing productive classroom climate.

Guidelines for Productive Classroom Climate

You should follow certain guidelines to establish a productive classroom climate and thereby avoiding disciplinary problems.

I. Know yourself: You should thoroughly understand your scope and limitations before going to teach.
II. Know your students: You should establish informal contact with your students and try to understand their ability, needs and background.
III. Know previous experience of students: You should know the past experience of your students before you are going to develop a new content area.
IV. Activities in classroom: You should begin the class naturally and proceed with the participation of students. You should be sincere, authentic and helpful to students while they are learning.

These guidelines will help you to establish a productive classroom climate. Now let us see how classroom climate influence classroom management.

Influence of Classroom Climate on Classroom Management

We have already discussed various factors contributing to classroom climate and guidelines for a productive classroom climate. The nature of classroom climate will have influence on discipline as we defined discipline as a process of self direction. In the process of self direction we must have respect to others and co-operate with others. Activities which are helpful for self direction and co-operation can be developed with good classroom climate. Thus, the students belonging to such classes will be disciplined as they get opportunity for development of discipline. So it is your duty to provide the classroom climate suitable for development of discipline. Where there is improper classroom climate, there will be indiscipline problems. Such problems will affect classroom management.

Summing Up

In this chapter, we have discussed the basic aspects of classroom management, discipline and major factors involved in classroom management. The major points of discussion can be summarised as follows.

1. Discipline is a dynamic process of self-direction.
2. Discipline has three stages of development, namely basic disciplinary stage, constructive stage and generative stage.
3. In basic disciplinary stage, children follow directions and teacher should encourage them to clarify their doubts.
4. In constructive stage, pupils are able to look co-operatively under the guidelines of teachers. Teacher should give more opportunity to their pupils to work co-operatively.
5. In generative stage, pupils are able to take up social responsibilities and teacher should give leadership opportunities to them.

6. An outstanding teacher has the following characteristics: Such teacher will be excellent in communication, expert in subject, excellent in teaching, always give priority to pupil's interest, responsible, systematic, stimulative and warm.
7. Characteristics of teachers have influence on classroom management is in two ways
   i. Factors influenced by teachers such as parent-teacher relationship, out of school activities, and administrative aspects.
   ii. Factors controlled by teachers are instruction, classroom management and evaluation.
8. Factors determining the nature of classroom climate are degree of formality, flexibility, structure, anxiety, teacher control and stimulation.
9. To establish a productive classroom climate you should know yourself, your students, previous experience of students, and to develop best set of instructional activities.
10. Discipline problems are unlikely to occur in classes with appropriate classroom climate.

CHAPTER 30

Problems in Classroom Management

Students belonging to different physical, social and psychological backgrounds are enrolled in our schools. So school is a place of conflict and compromise. Naturally problems arise due to the differences among pupils. These problems will give rise to indiscipline in classrooms. Solving of such problems are very essential for the appropriate development of discipline.

Indiscipline — Meaning

We have already seen that discipline is self directive and self controlling process. Indiscipline is diametrically opposite to concept of discipline. We teachers, usually misinterpret the term indiscipline. According to this view a classroom in which all students properly dressed, sit all right without making any noise is a disciplined class. But if we examine this class in the light of our definition of discipline, we will see that it is not a well disciplined class. One thing is correct that they are attending and obeying the orders of the teacher. They will be disciplined only if they get opportunity for self direction and self development. So, indiscipline develops from lack of attention and lack of opportunity for self development, self control and self direction.

Causes of Indiscipline

The major causes are physical, physiological, psychological, social and instructional.

Physical Causes

Physical causes mean any kind of physical disabilities causing disciplinary problems. The physical disabilities involve physically handicapped, mentally handicapped, hearing impaired and visually handicapped conditions. This kind of physical inadequacy will lead to indiscipline, because these will adversely affect attention and self direction.

Physiological Causes

Physiological causes are directly dependent on physiological needs of children. Physiological needs are the basic needs of human beings, which you might have heard of. Now let us see what the basic needs are. The basic physiological needs of students are need for food, clothing, seating, studying etc. A student who is not getting enough food cannot attend the class. It is the same thing happening in the case of those who lack suitable clothing, enough seating and studying facilities. So a student with unsatisfied basic needs could not acquire basic discipline. And now we pass on to the psychological causes of indiscipline.

Psychological Causes

Psychological causes of indiscipline arise from psychological problems. The major psychological problems involve problems of adolescents and self actualisation need of pupils. Since, secondary school pupils are at the beginning of adolescence, they will have problems of adolescence. The pupils at this stage are in role confusion. One and the same time they wish for attention getting and they are a little shy to take initiation in activities. The appearance of secondary sexual characteristics will also cause day dreaming and frustrations. At this stage, pupils will do many things knowingly or unknowingly to attract the opposite sex. Need for perfection or self actualisation is the ultimate need for a person. Each one strives to satisfy this need when all other needs are satisfied. All these psychological aspects will give rise to a number of indiscipline problems. Solving of such problems is very important as far as the further development of the individual is concerned.

Social Causes

Among the social causes acceptance, socialisation and social class are the three important problem areas. We know that classroom is a miniature society and has vital role in socialisation. Sharing of ideas and objects is very essential in classroom. Such give and take principle is the basis for socialisation. A more cared child or a single child may be poorly socialised and has some adjustment problems in the classroom. A better socialised child will get acceptance among the class mates very soon. A poorly socialised child will have some problems of acceptance. Along with these, the social class of the individual also is a determinant factor of social acceptance. There will be superiority and inferiority feelings among individuals of higher class and backward class respectively which will create acceptance and adjustment problems. All these social aspects will lead to indiscipline in classrooms. Here also you have to analyse the correct causes of indiscipline and solve it in the appropriate way. Now we shall pass on to the instructional causes of indiscipline.

Instructional Causes

Along with other causes, there are instructional causes of indiscipline also. Now let us see what the instructional causes of indiscipline are. We have already discussed about classroom climate and factors influencing classroom climate. There we noted that classroom climate and the characteristics of the teacher are very important as far as classroom discipline is concerned.

Consider a highly structured classroom with high formality and no flexibility. This will lead to many indiscipline problems. Sometimes learning activities are very easy and sometimes they are very tough. In both the cases pupils will have some problems. Excess teacher control curtails student's need for freedom which also causes certain problems of indiscipline.

These are the various instructional causes of indiscipline.

Overcoming the Causes of Indiscipline

Overcoming Physical Causes

First of all we have discussed the physical causes. You have to identify your pupils with any physical disability. There of course are special educational institutions for blind, deaf, dumb, etc. So you should identify orthopedically handicapped pupils and those with hearing and/ or visual disabilities. You should provide convenient seats for them and direct one or two pupils to help those children with special needs. You should also take care of those children from being teased by other children. These will help them to overcome inferiority.

Overcoming Physiological Causes

Secondly, we have discussed the physiological causes leading to indiscipline. Our basic needs are more profound among physiological causes. The basic needs are needs for food, dress, seating and studying facilities. Now let us think how we could overcome these causes. In our schools, mid-day meal program is going on for the benefit of children up to seventh standard. At the higher secondary level we have no such programmes. So, you may organise mid-day meal programme with local help for those who deserve it. Usually uniforms are common in our schools. So, if there is any pupil without proper dress, you could give them a set of dress using the school fund. Providing seating and studying facilities can be done more easily with the aid for enough furniture in classroom.

Overcoming Psychological Causes

The third cause we have discussed is the psychological causes. The most relevant cause in this category is role confusion among adolescents and their self actualisation need. Most of the psychological problems can be solved through counselling. You should act as a correct model in the adult role for your students. Their role confusion can be removed by making them participate in instructional activities and assigning them certain activities which they themselves can do. For example, you are going to arrange a field trip. Organisation of various aspects of the field trip can be assigned to small groups of students of your class. This type of participation will help your students to overcome their frustrations to a considerable extent. In addition to these, you should inquire into the causes of frustration and give them appropriate suggestions and assign suitable discipline developing activities. Along with these, involving them in creative works will help your pupils to realise the way to self actualisation. Once you win the approval and respect of the adolescents, then there will not be indiscipline problems in your classrooms.

Overcoming Social Causes

Now, we shall discuss about the ways to overcome social causes of indiscipline. The major problems are in relation to social acceptance and adjustment. You should adopt group activities for teaching selected topics to promote sharing mentality and respect for others in pupils. By taking part in such group activities pupils will be gradually socialised. They learn what their roles are, and how their work influences others and vice versa. So your duty as a teacher is to provide enough opportunity for pupils to work together. Sometimes, there may be students who are poorly socialised and having difficulty to work with others. They may be isolated children. With the help of other students they may be included in small groups and provide positive reinforcement and praising them as and when required, gradually they also can be socialised.

Overcoming Instructional Causes

Lastly we have discussed the instructional causes of indiscipline. Among these causes classroom climate and characteristics of teacher are the important influencing factors. The nature of classroom climate greatly depends on you. So you should design the classroom climate in such a way that it will maximise learning. You are the only authority who determines the structuring and formality of your class. The structure and formality should be low in order to reduce indiscipline problems. You should design instructional activities of various types, which will help you to cater to the needs of children with differing interests. You should make adequate changes in your teaching plan, if required. So you should design your classroom with less structure, low formality and adequate flexibility.

These suggestions will be helpful in overcoming the problems in classroom management.

Summing Up

In this chapter we have discussed the major causes of indiscipline and the ways to overcome each of the causes. The major points of our discussion can be summarised as follows.

1. Indiscipline means lack of attention and lack of self development, self control and self direction.
2. The major causes of indiscipline are
   a. physical causes – such as physical disabilities
   b. Physiological causes – such as unsatisfied basic needs
   c. Psychological causes – such as role confusion and unsatisfied strive for self actualisation.
   d. Social causes – such as less social acceptance and social stratification.
   e. Instructional causes – such as rigid classroom climate and unsuitable characteristics of teachers.
3 The way to overcome the causes of indiscipline are

a	Physical causes	-	to give special care
b	Physiological	-	to organise programmes to satisfy basic needs
c	Psychological	-	To give counselling and discipline developing activities
d	Social causes	-	To provide more group activities
e	Instructional causes	-	To provide productive classroom climate and establishing good support with pupils

4 Overcoming indiscipline problems will be helpful for better classroom management.

Chapter 31
Procedure of Classroom Management

Management of classroom activities is a headache to many of us. Both beginners and experienced teachers may have confronted with discipline problems in their professional life. Usually we try to maintain discipline in our own way. It may not have any systematic guidelines. In the previous chapter the different specific causes of indiscipline and its remedies were discussed. Here, we discuss certain general guidelines for better classroom management which will include those remedies, and criteria for selecting, the discipline developing activities have also been provided. This may be helpful in the professional life to develop skill in better classroom management.

Guidelines for Better Classroom Management

Elimination of physical distractions: Here physical distractions mean the physical facilities in classroom such as aeration, lighting, temperature and seating which are inadequate. The classroom would be arranged in such a way to get enough aeration, lighting and seating facilities. The chalk board would be placed in such a manner to avoid glare on it and visible for all in the class. Furniture should be placed in a manner to avoid a congestive nature to the classroom. You have to eliminate all such physical distractions in your classroom, before you are moving to the process of teaching.

Treat students with respect: Mahatma Gandhi said, "Child is the father of the man". In present day teaching, we must give more importance to learners. In the development of discipline you, the teacher, should act as an effective model. So you should treat pupils/learners with due respect. If you treat your pupils with respect, they will give respect to you in return. The respect, that you show to your pupils in turn, will encourage them to respect their classmates and elders in the society.

Seek students help in organising learning activity: As a teacher, your aim is to help pupils to reach the final stage of discipline. So you should give enough opportunity to your pupils to take part in organising and executing various learning activities. If they are involved in such activities, they will be more interested in learning. Holding of responsibilities in this way will help students to attain the final stage of development of discipline, that is, self direction.For example, you are going to teach parts of a flower. You can ask your students to bring different types of flowers to the classroom. Then ask them to separate different parts of flowers. Then ask them to compare the parts of different flowers. Likewise you should ensure participation of your students in learning activities.

Maintain expectation on students: Usually teachers have expectations on student's learning. We try to understand each pupil on the basis of their performance in classroom; we assure a certain level of achievement from them. Your students should know about your expectations on them. Knowledge of these expectations will prompt them for more learning and higher achievement. These expectations will help your children to be disciplined also.

Use variety of instructional procedure: Classroom with a single type of instructional procedure will make learning as a boring activity. You should adopt various instructional procedures in your classroom, with the co-operation of your students to cater to their interest. This will also help you to cater to individual differences as different individuals have interest in different activities. Once the pupils are interested in the learning activity, then there will not be discipline problems.For example, you can teach a lesson on Our Environment using lecture type presentation or more effectively by using procedure such as lecture, narration, discussion, experimentation and field study. Such type of multiple procedure is helpful to maintain classroom discipline.

Provision of appropriate feedback: You might have experienced that pupils demand for valued answer paper on the very next day of the test, what does this show? Of course, this is the indication of individuals' eagerness to have the knowledge of result. So you have to give immediate and appropriate feedback to your students. Periodical questioning (questioning in between the lesson relating to different objectives of the lesson) also will provide feedback to students. If you are not asking periodical questions, your students would think that learning of a particular area is not necessary. So be careful about your questioning. Periodical questioning prompts pupils to be attentive in the class, as they may have a question posed to them at any point of time. Naturally, this will reduce problems of indiscipline to a certain extent.

Provision of Positive Reinforcement: Positive enforcement is known to you. In simple terms, it means rewards. Usually we teachers always try to highlight the errors made by children. Actually it is an incorrect way, though we mean it for the good of the children. For example, Tom is a tenth standard student, who is good in mathematics. But in the half yearly examination he got only forty marks out of fifty in mathematics. Both the teacher and parents scolded him for his mistakes. But nobody cared for his achievements. This shocked him deeply, and he got only minimum marks required for a pass in mathematics in the next test.

From this example you can see the importance of positive reinforcement, or reward or praise. Certainly, simple praising will encourage your pupils generally for learning more effectively. So try to provide positive rewards as and when required. This will minimise your efforts considerably for reducing indiscipline problems.

Teacher must be consistent: It is said that an intelligent student can rate a teacher within the first ten minutes of the very first class. So, be vigilant in classrooms, because our pupils are more advanced in many respects than us. We know that one could build up a good image through months or years long strenuous effort, but everything can collapse within a moment or two. So, a teacher must be consistent in thought and action. If pupils (learners) know that you (teacher) are saying one thing and doing another thing, they will not respect you and discipline problems will emerge soon. So try to be more consistent, it helps you enjoy teaching.

Develop peer acceptance: We know that peer acceptance is one of the important factors in the life of individuals, especially adolescents. Usually a teacher can win the respect and approval of a majority of pupils in a classroom. An intelligent teacher is able to redirect pupils towards learning with the help of peers. For example, Joe is class teacher of X-B class. Majority of pupils respect him, but some of them are not in good term with him. One day he announced in the class that they needed a class leader and who would be the best choice. As planned earlier, most of the students approved Ramesh as their leader. Once he became leader, Ramesh became a well disciplined student.

From this example we can see that peer approval has vital importance in avoiding or solving discipline problems. So remember that once majority of students are with you, you can bring all of them towards you by using certain tactics and be able to avoid problems in classrooms.

Training for pupils: In many occasions of teaching life, you might have seen that pupils work disorderly. What can you do at these times? You should give necessary training for students. For example, it is the time for morning assembly and your students are going for assembly in zig zag manner and talking to each other. What will you do? You can call them back and ask them to go in a straight line without making any noise. You should also give training in this regard. Likewise you shall train them at proper occasions to avoid creating problems. But at times we may have to use punishment. Punishment is the last resort for maintaining discipline. Instead of punishment you should give one more chance to the pupils, which will help them to develop proper behaviour through training. So, you should design your teaching plan in such a way to avoid discipline problems.

Discipline Developing Activities

Pupils with discipline problems can be seen in any classroom. So, it is essential for you to know some of the discipline developing activities which are given to pupils with discipline problems. The rationale behind these activities is redirection of destructive behaviour into socially useful behaviour. Actually this redirection is the socialisation process. Now let us discuss some of the discipline developing activities.

Model of discipline developing activities

These include individual and group activities of different durations. Some of the activities are discussed as follows:

1. *Construction of Notice Board and Bullettin Board:* This will be an excellent and time consuming activity. While making these, pupils will have to work cooperatively and logically
2. *Design poster, collect pictures and news clippings:* This is another useful activity that can follow the first activity. You should ask pupils to design posters on selected topics and to collect pictures and news clippings related to the given topic. For example, topics such as pollution, deforestation, health and sanitation, animal conservation, etc. can be given.
3. *Preparation of learning aids:* You have to prepare different learning aids as per the content to be taught. You can seek the participation of your pupils in preparing learning aids. In this regard, you should give necessary directions to students. Participation in such activities help pupils to learn more meaningfully.
4. *Preparation and maintenance of accessory learning aids:* Preparation and maintaining accessory learning aids such as aquarium, terrarium, green house and vegetable garden is a very effective discipline developing activity.
5. *Develop working plan for field study:* You know that field study is an essential part of biology teaching. In order to conduct effective field study, it is essential to develop suitable plan of action. You should ask your pupils to make a list of places to where field trips can be conducted. You can also direct them to develop working plan for field trip to each of such selected places.
6. *Framing of questions:* You should ask pupils to frame questions on selected topics, preferably on the lessons which are already covered. This will help them to learn more easily and meaningfully.
7. Preparation of handwritten magazines: Preparation of handwritten magazines is essentially a very good activity leading towards the proper development of discipline. You can suggest one subject for

each edition or allow your students to propose one. You may edit the articles and the writing should be assigned to pupils who are having good handwriting.

8. Organisation of peer teaching: You might have heard of peer teaching. It is a very good activity to foster discipline in your classrooms. A group of students are selected in advance and assigned with teaching of certain topics, either to groups or to individual on the basis of the toughness of the lesson. This will help to increase the interest of students in learning and help them to clarify many of their doubts.
9. *Voluntary activities:* It is proved that voluntary activities will help to develop discipline to a greater extent. A variety of voluntary activities can be organised in school with the help of students. Some of such activities are organising sports, celebration of important national days, cleaning school surroundings or play ground preparing garden, etc. Such activities help to foster service mindedness in children.

These are some of the major discipline development activities. You can develop such activities as per the needs of your pupils and institution. While adopting activities you should consider the following as the criteria for organising discipline developing activities.

Criteria for Selecting Discipline Developing Activities

Now let us see the important criteria for selecting, discipline developing activities. There are five important criteria for selecting discipline developing activities. *The activities should be structured; activities should be according to interest, number of students and toughness of activity. Activities should be relevant and the result of the activity should be seen.*

Now let us see those criteria one by one.

1. *Activities should be structured:* Structuring means planning almost all activities up to the completion of the activity meant for development of discipline. Structuring is very important, because we were dealing with pupil's need to develop discipline. So, the activities provided should be well organieed. For example, you are asking to compose questions on the topic 'sense organs'. For the sake of convenience, groups are formed. Separate sections of the topic are given to each group. Then ask them to read the given portion, have a discussion on it and to frame different types of questions. You should also make them aware of the need to find out the answer while they frame each question. This kind of structuring will help pupils to proceed correctly.
2. *Number of student and toughness of activity:* The number of students needed to work on a given activity depends on the toughness of the

activity. Too many students on a simple activity and very few students on a tough activity will not serve the purpose of the activity. So the number of pupils per activity should be determined. For example, in the case of developing a working plan for field study, the whole class can be divided into group of five to eight students and duties should be assigned to each group. This shall include making list of places, determining transport facilities, objectives of the trip, arrangement of food and collection of materials. The question framing activity discussed above can even be assigned as individual work also.

So you should take care of the number of students needed to work on each activity before students are exposed to various activities.

3. *Activity should be according to the interest:* We know that certain children do not like certain activity. So, while assigning the activities, interest of children should be taken into consideration. Give a chance to them to select activity as per their choice.
4. *Activity should be relevant*: We have already discussed the major activities. While selecting an activity you should match the relevance of the activity with the ability and the level of your pupils. Activities which are irrelevant will bring about negative attitude in pupils.
5. *Children would see the result of the Activity:* We know that the knowledge of results is a crucial factor in the life of an individual. It is not merely confined to examinations, but with various aspects of daily life. Here while pupils select an activity that you assigned, the termination point would be more pleasurable and rewarding, if they can see the result of their work and get appreciation from others about that work. For example, your pupils prepare and maintain an aquarium in the classroom. Naturally pupils from other classes and teachers will come and observe it. This will be the greatest reward for your pupils and this encourages them to do more complicated activities in future life.

These are the various criteria while you are selecting a discipline developing activity.

Summing Up

Guidelines for better classroom management, discipline developing activities and criteria for selecting discipline developing activities are discussed. The major points of our discussion can be summarised as follows.

I. The major guidelines for classroom management are as follows:
    - eliminate physical distractions treat students with respect
    - seek students help in organising learning activities
    - maintain expectation on students

- use variety of instructional procedure
- provision of appropriate feedback
- provision of positive reinforcement
- teacher must be consistent
- develop peer acceptance
- training for pupils.

II) Some discipline developing activities are helpful in maintaining discipline.

The major discipline developing activities are:

i) Make notice board and bulletin board
ii) Make posters, collect pictures and news clips.
iii) Preparation of learning aids
iv) Preparation of and maintaining accessory learning aids
v) Develop working plan for field study
vi) Compose questions
vii) Preparation of hand written magazines
viii) Organise peer teaching and
ix) Voluntary activities.

III) There are certain criteria for selecting discipline developing activities, they are:

- Activities should be structured to get optimum results
- Number of students required to work per activity should be predetermined
- Activities should be according to the interest of the pupils
- Activity should be relevant to the age and ability of pupils
- Children should get the result of their activity, which will help to encourage them greatly.

References

Ary, D. Jacob, L. C & Razariah, A. (1972). *Introduction to Research in Education*. New York: Holt Rinehart & Winston Inc.

Bichler, R. F (1974). *Psychology applied to teaching*. Boston: Houghton Mifflin Co.

Blair, G. M. & John, R. S., and Simson, R. H. (1975). *Educational Psychology*. New York: Macmillan.

Bloom, B.S. (1979). *Taxonomy of Educational Objectives*. London: Longman Group.

Brog, N .R. & Gall, M. D. (1983). *Educational Research an Introduction*. New York: Longman.

Brow. J.W., Lewis, R. B. & Harcleroad, E. E. (1973). *AV Instruction, Technology, Media & Methods*. New York: McGraw Hill.

Cable, R. (1970). *Audio-Visual Handbook*. London: University of London

Cairy, C. M. (1988). *Measuring and Evaluating School Learning*. Boston: Allyn & Bacon Inc.

Dececo, J. P & Crawford. W. R. (1977). *Psychology of Learning and Instruction*.

Divesta, F. J & Thompson. G. G. (1970). *Educational Psychology*. New York: McGraw Hill.

Dressel, P. L. (1976). *Handbook of Academic Evaluation*. London: Jossy Bass Pub.

Driver, R., Asoko, H., Leach, J., Mortimer, E. & Scott, P. (1994). Constructing Scientific Knowledge in the Classroom', *Educational Researcher*, 23(7), 5-12.

Ebel, R. L. & Fransbie, D. A. (1991). *Essentials of Educational Measurement*. New Delhi: PHI.

Falk, D. (1971). *Biology Teaching Methods*. New York: John Wiley & Sons.

Goldmann, L. (1978). *Research Methods for Counsellors*. New York: John Wiley & Sons.

Hang, M. C., Reynolds, M. C. & Walberg, H. J. (1990). *Special Education Research and Practice*. Oxford: Pergamon Press.

Hurlock, E.B. (1973). *Adolescent Development*. London : McGraw Hill.

Joyce, B. & Weil, M. (1985). *Models of Teaching* (2nd edn). New Delhi: PHI.

Klinkmann, E. (1971). *Biology Teacher's Handbook*. New Delhi: Wiley Eastern.

Leach, J., & Scott, P. (2003). Individual and Sociocultural Views of Learning in *Science Education, Science & Education*, 12, 91-113.

Lindgran, H. C. (1976). *Educational Psychology in the Classroom*. New York: John Wiley & Sons.

Mason, E.J. & Bramble, W. J. (1988). *Understanding and Conducting Research*. New York: McGraw Hill.

Mathur, L. M. (1975). *Science Projects and School Science Projects*. New Delhi: University of Delhi.

Mehrens, W. A. & Lehman, I. J (1978). *Measurement and Evaluation in Education and Psychology*. New York: Holt Rinehart & Winston Pub.

Merholt, F., Wein, B. P. F., & Joseph, A (1988). *A Sourcebook for Biological Sciences*. Brace & World Inc.

Millman, J. & Hammond, L. D. (1990). *The New Handbook of Teacher Evaluation.* New Delhi: Sage.

Morse, W. C. & Wingo, G. M. (1968). *Psychology and Teaching*. Bombay: Tarapurwala & Sons.

Nair, C.P.S. (1971). *Teaching in Your Schools*. New Delhi

Nedelsky, L. (1965). *Science Teaching and testing*. New York: Harcourt Brace & World Inc.

Nunnally, J. C & Ator, N. A. (1972). *Educational Measurement and Evaluation.* New York: McGraw Hill.

Passi, J. C., Singh, L. C. & Sansanwal (1987). *Inquiry Training Model of Teaching.* Agra: National Psychological Corp.

Piaget, J. (1952). *The Origins of Intelligence in Children.* New York: International Universities Press.

Piaget, J. (1970). Piaget's theory. In P.H. Mussen (Ed.) *Carmichael's manual of child psychology* (3rd ed., pp. 703–732). New York: Wiley.

Pierce, W. D. & Lorber, M.A. (1971). *Objectives and Methods of Secondary Teaching.* New Jersey: PHI.

Reily. R. R. & Lewis, E. L. (1983). *Educational Psychology*. Canada: Collier Macmillan.

Ross, A.O. (1977). *Learning Disabilities*. New York: McGraw Hill.

Sayal, N. K. (1977). *Science Education*. New Delhi: S. Chand & Co.

Schwab, J. J. (1965). *Biology Teachers Handbook*. BSCS. New York: John Wiley & Sons.

Sharma, R.C. (1981). *Modern Science Teaching*. New Delhi: Oxford & IBH.

Srivastava, H S (2014). *Curriculum and Methods of Teaching*. Delhi: Shipra Publications.

Taber, Keith S. (2006). Beyond constructivism: the progressive research programme into learning science. *Studies in Science Education, 42,125-184.*

Tanner, L. N. (1978). *Classroom Discipline*. New York: Holt Rinehart & Winston.

Vygotsky, L. S. (1978). Tool and symbol in child development. In M. Cole, V. John-Steiner, S. Scribner, & E. Souberman (Eds.). *Mind in Society: The development of higher psychological processes*. Cambridge, Mass: Harvard University Press.

Washton, N.S. (1976). *Teaching Science Creatively*. London: W.B. Saunders & Co.

Weiner, F. (1973). *Help for the Handicapped Child.* USA: McGraw Hill

Weiner, I. B. & Elkind, D. (1972). *Readings in Child Development*. London: John Wiley & Sons.

Yip D. Y. (1998). Identification of misconceptions in novice biology teachers and remedial strategies for improving biology learning. *International Journal of Science Education,* 20(4), 461-477.